WALTER "SKIP" OLSEN
AND
WILLIAM "BILL" SOMMERS, PH.D.

A TRAINER'S COMPANION

STORIES TO STIMULATE
REFLECTION
CONVERSATION
ACTION

D1411575

Olsen, Walter, & Sommers, William A.
    A Trainer's Companion: Stories to Stimulate Reflection, Conversation, Action
        117 pp.
        ISBN 1-929229-39-9

1. Education   2. Leadership   3. Title

"The Twenty-Eighth Floor" by Kenneth Wydro. Copyright © 1980 by Kenneth Wydro. From *Think on Your Feet: The Art of Thinking and Speaking Under Pressure* by Kenneth Wydro, Prentice Hall, 1981. Reprinted by permission of the author.

"Fire and Water" reprinted by permission of *Harvard Business Review.* From "Parables of Leadership" by W. Chan Kim and Renée A. Mauborgne. July-August 1992. Copyright © 1992 by the Harvard Business School Publishing Corporation; all rights reserved.

"Cleaning Sidewalks" by Barry Oshry. Copyright © 1995 by Barry Oshry. From *Seeing Systems: Unlocking the Mysteries of Organizational Life,* Berret-Koehler Publishers, Inc., 1996. Reprinted by permission of the publisher.

"Epilogue: A Soft Answer" from *Safe and Alive* by Terry Dobson. Copyright © 1982 by Terry Dobson. Used by permission of Jeremy P. Tarcher, an imprint of Penguin Group (USA), Inc.

"The Wisdom of the Mountain" reprinted by permission of *Harvard Business Review.* From "Parables of Leadership" by W. Chan Kim and Renée A. Mauborgne. July-August 1992. Copyright © 1992 by the Harvard Business School Publishing Corporation; all rights reserved.

"Rule Number 6" reprinted by permission of Harvard Business School Press. From *The Art of Possibility: TransformingProfessional and Personal Life* by Rosamund Stone Zander and Benjamin Zander. Boston, MA 2000 Pp 79. Copyright © 2000 by Rosamund Stone Zander and Benjamin Zander, all rights reserved.

"The Story of the Five Balls" from *Suzanne's Diary for Nicholas* by James Patterson. Copyright © 2001 by SueJack, Inc. By permission of Little, Brown and Company, Inc.

"The Rabbi's Gift" as it appears in M. Scott Peck's Prologue from *The Different Drum: Community Making and Peace* (New York: Simon & Schuster, Inc. 1987). Reprinted by permission of the publisher.

"A System Trapped" by Peter Senge. Copyright © 1999 by Peter Senge. From *Schools That Learn: A Fifth Discipline Fieldbook for Parents, Educators, and Everyone Who Cares About Education,* Doubleday, 2000. Reprinted by permission of the author.

"The Chrysalis" reprinted with permission of Simon & Schuster Adult Publishing Group from *Report to Greco* by Nikos Kazantzakis. Translated from the Greek by P.A. Bien. English translation copyright © 1985 by Simon & Schuster, Inc.

"Autobiography in Five Chapters" by Portia Nelson. Copyright © 1993 by Beyond Words Publishing, Inc. From *There's a Hole in My Sidewalk: The Romance of Self-Discovery,* Beyond Words Publishing, Inc., 1994. Reprinted by permission of the publisher.

TABLE OF CONTENTS

ACKNOWLEDGMENTS

This book represents our labor of love for stories. As we have used stories in our classes and training sessions, we have seen the power of stories to create the containers for new thinking. We are grateful to many people who have contributed to our success and want to mention a number of them here.

I (Skip) wish to acknowledge a special group of "learning omnivores" who continue to confront knotty issues of leadership and learning and help me to see more clearly: Michael Ayers, Louise Covert, Ellen Debe, David Evelo, Sara Gjerdrum, Kay Gregory, Tom Heuerman, John Kostouros, Norm Moen, Ron Petrich, Jim Roussin, and Tom Siebold. I owe an enormous debt to Angeles Arrien and Patrick O'Neill, who taught me the power of music and story. Bill, a big thank you; I continue to enjoy your questions, points of view, and (mostly) your laughter. Finally, thanks to my wife, Janet, whose counsel and closeness make everything possible.

I (Bill) wish to acknowledge Dr. Art Costa for his coaching, mentoring, and guidance the past 20 years. Art and Dr. Bob Garmston are storytellers extraordinaire. Special thanks to Jane Stevenson and Marney Wamsley, who keep teaching me a great deal about leadership, integrity, and courage; to Pat Wolfe and Dennis Sparks, who impact my thinking about learning and organizations; to Michael Ayers and Tom Heuerman, who continue to challenge me with new concepts, business applications to education, and risk taking to produce better results; and to Diane Zimmerman and Dave Schumaker for their friendship, coaching, and learning together. Ruby Payne has been supportive, creative, and willing to push the boundaries in order to help all students learn. Finally, Skip, you are an amazing person to work with, and I am grateful for our collaborations.

Both of us would like to recognize Education Minnesota and the TALL (Teachers as Leaders and Learners) project for allowing us to work with teachers in Minnesota. In particular, we want to thank Sara Gjerdrum, Marcia Averbook, Garnet Franklin, Pat Reisenger, and Janelle Warner at Education Minnesota for their thoughtful conversations and assistance. We, of course, are indebted to the countless storytellers – some living, some no longer with us – behind the 25 stories in this book. We stand on their shoulders! Finally, we appreciate the folks at **aha!** Process, Inc. for their extraordinary help in publishing our work.

Walter "Skip" Olsen

William "Bill" Sommers

INTRODUCTION

God so loved stories that he created man.
–Quoted in Roland Barth's *Learning by Heart*

Our goal in life is to gather all the awareness one can, and then to pass it out freely to those who are interested.

–Manitonquat, Keeper of the Lore for the Assonet Band of Wampanoag Nation

WHY STORIES ARE IMPORTANT

This is a great question for leaders. Many business leaders and consultants (Michael Fullan, David Whyte, James Autry, Max DuPree, Peter Block, Robert Bly, and Roland Barth – to name just a few) believe that stories help create positive working climates for many reasons.

Stories create openings for people to talk and think, to wonder and reflect on their work and workplace. Stories help create healthy rituals, knit personal meaning, and build community by sustaining common experiences and language. The stories told in communities help initiate newcomers, provide operational norms, and pass on the kinds of historical understandings that serve as the underpinnings for cultural wisdom. This can be positive or negative, depending on how behavior is demonstrated based on the story.

The stories in this collection provide personal insight to understand change, to develop a healthy balance between work and personal life, to deal with conflict, to promote diversity, and to reframe traditionally negative experiences into positive opportunities. The stories herein will reinforce democratic values in the learning community because we all talk as peers, leaders, and co-workers.

Stories become a form of shorthand that represents what fables and myths once did in many human cultures. Think of phrases like "crying wolf," "opening Pandora's box," or "Achilles heel." Storytelling facilitates an exploration of organizational values and helps people identify and articulate what is important and meaningful. Think of how stories have been used – and are still being used – in indigenous cultures. They transmit beliefs and values to young and old alike.

Stories can prompt insight into knotty problems and challenges, as well as create new openings for change and growth. Alan M. Webber, founding editor of *Fast Company* magazine, notes that increased productivity and effectiveness in organizations often are the results of frequent conversations.

It's important to us that our workplaces include deeper, older wisdom about life and the way things are – "code," in effect, for the deeper, often hidden or unappreciated dynamics of life. Stories open windows into these misty and mysterious aspects of life. These stories and sayings "articulate the intuitive" and are enjoyable ways to captivate people and interest them in what is significant in their work and lives. They provide powerful and innovative ways of seeing situations and alternative ways of seeing issues. This shift in gears helps reframe situations, people, problems, and challenges. Pathways open for us to take action as we awaken from our daily thinking patterns to a more conscious, mindful way of being with difficulties.

Stories help us connect the heart and the head while inviting us to consider additional dimensions of life that are often ignored: commitment, feelings, aesthetics, ethics, and spirituality. Stories engage the right hemisphere of the brain, eliciting holistic approaches that sometimes lie dormant in our data-based world. The press and rush of the oft-frenetic workday muffle the subtle, softer realities. Stories pierce the foggy veil to build pathways for creativity and wonder, for imagination and nonlinear thinking.

Our aim here is to build the individual and organizational capacity to communicate, practice dialogue, and sustain collaborative group processes. Practicing new and different ways of talking to one another helps widen perspectives and incorporate diverse thoughts. It also can lead to collaborative problem solving.

We often think of stories as being for children. Yet we have found that adult learners, rich in experience and insight, can easily relate to the point or moral of a story. Recall the last workshop you attended. What do you remember most vividly? The research or the stories? What has had a longer-term impact on you – stories or data?

Stories offer bite-sized learning experiences that are short and to the point; they frequently come to us in metaphor. As Bob Samples wrote years ago in *The Metaphoric Mind,* the brain processes information using metaphors. Stories are a familiar cultural form. We attend plays and movies that tell stories; we read stories to our children and tell stories at the water cooler; and we're engaged with stories in the news, magazines, and popular books.

Welcome to the world of stories. Use them well, and do good work.

Skip Olsen
Bill Sommers

WHAT'S IN THIS BOOK?

We've organized the stories into categories based on themes that are of paramount importance in workplaces:

- Reframing
- Diversity
- Conflict
- Balance
- Change

Each section's introduction contains a general overview of the issue, resources for deeper understanding, and pertinent quotations that you might use for additional activities or discussions. The point is to make explicit the resources that are readily available on the Web for further study or to enrich discussions. For example, many of the articles cited could be used for study circles or jigsaw activities (e.g., individuals summarizing particular readings for the larger group). Many of the books lend themselves to book clubs at school or the workplace, promoting both learning and collegiality.

Each story is introduced with a brief discussion about why we see the story as pertinent to important issues in any organization. There is space to note why you are choosing the story to read now; why does the story fit with your work now? As you develop a familiarity with the stories, you will see connections between them and possibilities for their use with other groups and situations.

Stories are best when they come from the heart with passion and energy. They are constructive in nature and offer possibilities. This will help you see or create many more stories. Make notes to develop your own journal and to refine your practice. Insights are sometimes like a meteor in your peripheral vision: While you didn't see it clearly, you are certain something bright and glowing was there. Make notes often, or you risk forgetting important discoveries.

Ideas will come in at least two ways. First, when you read the story yourself in preparation, connections will become apparent. Second, as you go through the story with other learners, questions and differing interpretations will add even more ideas. It's important that the process be as developmental and reflective as possible in order to leverage the full power of the stories in your learning community.

ARTWORK AND SYMBOLS

The artwork on our pages is intentional and important. We include the art of indigenous people because of its symbolic nature and relation to our work. It's a reminder that we're going back to the deeper ideas of community at the core of humans living together.

 The circle on the Introduction page represents the journey all of us are on – a finite journey, with a beginning and an end. It's a reminder that our time is limited and acting on what matters most is vitally important.

 The winged figure that marks every "Resources for Deeper Understanding" section is a dragonfly that frequently represents growth. It helps us communicate our desire that you deepen your understanding of the issues at hand.

The diamond-shaped figure that sets off the title of the stories represents the insights or wisdom of the shaman. Hence, we associate that symbol with the wisdom in the stories.

Kokopelli, the Anasazi flute player, is the trickster, the master of surprise, laughter, and the sensual. Clearly, Kokopelli would love stories and might even join in with his music to give us more to think about!

The hand is associated with the guiding questions and conversation surrounding the story. It's a reminder of how much energy and new learning we create along the way when we work with something. It's with hands that we work life: We touch each other, we create art and conduct symphonies, we cradle our young.

The circle of human beings connected to one another on the title page is based on the design of the Washington Covenant Belt (Iroquois), which was used as a covenant of peace between the 13 original United States colonies and the Six Nations. It symbolizes for us our interdependence.

WHAT IF ...

Playing with "what if" statements is a healthy way to gain insight into possibilities and alternatives. The story and the perceptions about your environment get worked from different angles with different insights and values when you ask "what if ..." We've posed two "what if" questions for each story to help you start the process. We urge you to use these and also to create your own during discussion. What different endings might there be? What ending would you like to see? Why? How do you combine differently? What other possibilities exist? Which "what if" questions jump out at you?

REFRAMING:
THE ART OF SEEING DIFFERENTLY

The world of education is a very difficult place to work these days. As a matter of fact, it's getting more difficult each year. There are increased demands, reduction in funding, and more vocal criticism of what educators are doing.

People who choose to be professional educators want to make a difference in the lives of young people. Educators want to help students learn, to prepare them for a productive and fulfilling life; they genuinely want to do the best by students and their families. Despite the noble intentions and hard work, however, business, government, the media, and other members of our communities are increasingly critical of schools and educators. While some of the ideas are welcome and helpful, many are not. Some are selfish, one-dimensional, and "crazy-makers" for schools and educators. When we can't control other people's actions but are held responsible for the consequences, the double bind keeps many staff members stuck in powerless situations.

A similar thing can happen to students. U.S. research professor Martin Seligman, author of *Learned Optimism,* writes about learned helplessness. Enthusiasm wanes and depression occurs when children or adults perceive life as not going well and feel that the condition is permanent, hopeless.

Reframing helps people continue to work, even with negative feedback. When we change the game we're playing, sometimes those attacking us don't know how to adapt. Reframing has been used both as a therapeutic process and a creative-thinking skill. The process involves looking at an issue from different perspectives. People are energized by seeing things differently, recognizing more options, and creating capacity to take positive actions.

When people start seeing problems from another point of view, they begin having an optimistic attitude that fosters even more change. British educational consultant and author Edward de Bono believes that creativity is the most important skill to develop. Business leaders look for creative people because they understand that innovation in developing new products is the lifeblood of a company's success.

The following stories will provide a few examples of reframing – to be used with staff, students, and community.

RESOURCES FOR DEEPER UNDERSTANDING

♦ **ARTICLES**

NSDC (National Staff Development Council) Library: School Culture available at >http://www.nsdc.org/library/school.html<. Here's a sample of articles that have been available. Titles change from time to time. Of course, all are available online with a membership in NSDC – highly recommended. The articles are generally shorter (appropriate for busy educators) and useful (in both content and process) for various staff development requirements.

DuFour, Rick, & Burnette, Becky. (2002). Pull out negativity by its roots. *Journal of Staff Development* (PDF version). Summer.

Hirsh, Stephanie. (1996). Creating a healthy school culture is everyone's business. *Innovator*. October.

Pardini, Priscilla. (2002). Stitching new teachers into the school's fabric. *Journal of Staff Development* (PDF version). Summer.

Peterson, Kent D. (2002). Positive or negative. *Journal of Staff Development* (PDF version). Summer.

Richardson, Joan. (1999). Harness the potential of staff meetings. *Tools for Schools*. October/November.

Richardson, Joan. (1996.) School culture: a key to improved student learning. *Innovator*. October.

Richardson, Joan. (2001). Shared culture. *Results*. May.

Student learning grows in professional cultures. (1998). *Tools for Schools*. August/September.

♦ **THE BOOKSHELF**

Dauten, Dale. (1996). *The Max Strategy.* New York, NY: William Morrow & Co.

de Bono, Edward. (1970). *Lateral Thinking.* New York, NY: Harper & Row.

Goldberg, Marilee C. (1998). *The Art of the Question.* New York, NY: John Wiley & Sons.

Gordon, David. (1978). *Therapeutic Metaphors.* Cupertino, CA: Meta Publications.

Hay, Louise L. (1991). *The Power Is Within You.* Carson, CA: The Hay House.

Johnson, Spencer. (1998). *Who Moved My Cheese?* New York, NY: Penguin Putnam.

Juster, Norton. (1961). *The Phantom Tollbooth.* New York, NY: Bullseye Books.

Kegan, Robert, & Lahey, Lisa Laskow. (2001). *How the Way We Talk Can Change the Way We Work.* San Francisco, CA: Jossey-Bass.

Siegel, Bernie. (1986). *Love, Medicine, and Miracles.* New York, NY: HarperCollins.

Seligman, Martin E.P. (1990). *Learned Optimism.* New York, NY: Alfred A. Knopf.

Zander, Benjamin, & Zander, Rosamund Stone. (2000). *The Art of Possibility.* Boston, MA: Harvard Business School Press.

◆ USEFUL QUOTATIONS

By adopting strength-based paradigms, we clearly separate negative behavior from a person's worth. In fact, we frequently can scrutinize the problem behavior and discover strengths that lie beneath the obvious weaknesses. This is called reframing:

driven?	no, energetic!
stubborn?	no, determined!
bizarre?	no, creative!
rebellious?	no, independent!
obsessive?	no, organized!
delusional?	no, imaginative!

By reframing negative attributions into positive potentials, we plant a seed and nurture it. Such is our business.

–Joseph Burger, U.S. professor and writer

He who sleeps in continual noise is wakened by silence.

–W.D. Howells, U.S. writer

It is easier to get forgiveness than it is to secure permission.

–Jesuit saying

It takes nine months to have a baby, no matter how many people you put on the job.

–North American saying

Many a man would rather you heard his story than granted his request.

–Phillip Stanhope, fourth earl of Chesterfield, England

The beginning of wisdom is to call things by their right names.

–Chinese proverb

Almost anything is easier to get into than out of.

–Agnes Allen, U.S. epigrammatist

Just because everything is different doesn't mean that anything has changed.

–Irene Peter, U.S. epigrammatist

A rock pile ceases to be a rock pile the moment a single man contemplates it, bearing within him the image of a cathedral.

–Antoine de Saint-Exupery, French novelist

The opposite of an ordinary fact is a lie. But the opposite of one profound truth may be another profound truth.

–Niels Bohr, Danish physicist

It is tempting to think up futures that don't require getting there from here.

–Harlan Cleveland, U.S. essayist and lecturer

Between what I think,
What I want to say,
What I believe I'm saying,
What I say,
What you want to hear,
What you hear,
What you believe you understand,
What you want to understand,
And what you understood,
There are at least nine possibilities for misunderstanding.

–Francois Garagnon, French jurist

Where you stumble, there your treasure lies.

–Joseph Campbell, U.S. author and mythologist

All of us, whether or not we are warriors, have a cubic centimeter of chance that pops out in front of our eyes from time to time. The difference between an average man and a warrior is that the warrior is aware of this, and one of his tasks is to be alert, deliberately waiting, so that when his cubic centimeter pops out he has the necessary speed, the prowess, to pick it up.

–Carlos Castaneda, Mexican anthropologist and author

Something we were withholding made us weak
Until we found it was ourselves.

–Robert Frost, U.S. poet

Things never were "the way they used to be."
Things never will be "the way it's going to be someday."
Things are always just the way they are for the time being.
And the time being is always in motion.

–Alexander Evangeli Xenopouloudakis, character in a novel in progress by Robert Fulghum

We shouldn't try to do something better until we first determine if we should do it at all.

–Dwight D. Eisenhower, 34th U.S. president

No problem can be solved from the same consciousness that created it.

–Albert Einstein, German/Swiss/U.S. physicist

Spectacular achievements are always preceded by unspectacular preparation.

–Roger Staubach, National Football League quarterback

Nobody sees a flower, really – it is so small – we haven't time, and to see takes time, like to have a friend takes time.

–Georgia O'Keefe, U.S. artist

The little things? The little moments? They aren't little.

–John Kabat-Zinn, U.S. professor and author

Spend the afternoon. You can't take it with you.

–Annie Dillard, U.S. writer

Whether you think you can or think you can't, you're right.

–Henry Ford, U.S. industrialist

Plans are only good intentions unless they immediately degenerate into hard work.

–Peter Drucker, Austrian/U.S. author and business consultant

Failure is only the opportunity to begin again more intelligently.

–Henry Ford, U.S. industrialist

Actions lie louder than words.

–Carolyn Wells, U.S. author

Believe those who are seeking the truth. Doubt those who find it.

–André Gide, French novelist

Everybody gets so much information all day long that they lose their common sense.

—Gertrude Stein, U.S./French writer

The reverse side also has a reverse side.

—Japanese proverb

The test of a first-rate intelligence is the ability to hold two opposed ideas in the mind at the same time, and still retain the ability to function.

—F. Scott Fitzgerald, U.S. novelist

◈ 'HOW ARE THE CHILDREN?' ◈

WHY THIS STORY?

Educators are working hard – overworking in many cases. Sometimes during the hustle and bustle of school operations, district issues, and community problems, educators are diverted from their purpose. The vision is blurred or forgotten altogether. It is important to remember why we are working hard and giving more than is required. As Austrian author and Holocaust survivor Viktor Frankl said, "We can live with the how if we know the why."

An antidote to this organizational blood poisoning is articulating frequently a clear purpose to focus staff, students, and community on learning.

This story is an example of how a community can keep a major concept in mind during the daily grind. This culture transmits a primary goal through oral communication. As you read the story, you will understand how the important outcomes are kept alive, distributed through daily conversations, and discussed.

Begin by reading the story yourself. Decide whether you will use the story in your training. Make some notes about how the story does or does not fit with your work at this time. You also might want to expand on the ideas above.

_____

_____

_____

_____

_____

_____

_____

_____

_____

_____

THE STORY: 'HOW ARE THE CHILDREN?'

Among the many accomplished and fabled tribes of Africa, no tribe was considered to have warriors more fearsome or more intelligent than the mighty Masai. It is perhaps surprising then to learn the traditional greeting that passed between Masai warriors. "Kasserian ingera," one would always say to another. It means "And how are the children?"

It is still the traditional greeting among the Masai, acknowledging the high value that the Masai place on their children's well-being. Even warriors with no children of their own would always give the traditional answer, "All the children are well." This meant, of course, that peace and safety prevail; that the priorities of protecting the young and the powerless are in place; that the Masai people have not forgotten their reason for being, their proper function, and their responsibilities. "All the children are well" means that life is good. It means that the daily struggles of existence, even among a poor people, include the proper care of the young and defenseless.

I wonder how it might affect our consciousness or our own children's welfare if, in our own culture, we took to greeting each other with the same daily question, "And how are the children?" I wonder if we heard that question and passed it along to each other a dozen times a day, if it would begin to make a difference in the reality of how children are thought of or cared for in this country …

I wonder what it would be like if every adult among us – parents and non-parents alike – felt an equal weight of responsibility for the daily care and protection of all the children in our town, in our state, in our country. I wonder if we could truly say without hesitation, "The children are well; yes, all the children are well."

What would it be like? If the president began every press conference, every public appearance, by answering the question: "And how are the children, Mr. President?" If every governor of every state had to answer the same question at every press conference: "And how are the children, Governor? Are they well?"

Wouldn't it be interesting to hear their answers?

QUESTIONS TO CONSIDER

1. How important is it to ask that question often? To what extent do we agree around here on the answer to that question?

2. What would be *your* answer to the greeting? Why would you answer that way?

3. If the Masai answered that the children are well, it meant that "peace and safety prevail; that the priorities of protecting the young and the powerless are in place; that the Masai people have not forgotten their reason for being, their proper function, and their responsibilities." How does that strike you as a definition of well-being? What would you add? What might be your descriptor for kids in school?

4. How might people from different segments of North American society answer the question?

5. What is transmitted in your organization orally?

6. How do you keep the goals of the organization in the minds of your colleagues?

WHAT IF ...

1. We shared this story with our larger community?

2. Kids offered an answer to this question?

NOTES TO MYSELF

_____

_____

_____

_____

_____

_____

MY GRANDFATHER'S STORY
(TWO WOLVES)

WHY THIS STORY?

Educators are seasonal workers. In the fall, school starts with exuberant energy and excitement. The holiday season offers a diversion and a chance to renew energy. As winter drags on, January and February bring difficulty to work and relationships. Conversations turn to what is wrong, budget cuts, and what hasn't been covered. In many places, people have been inside because of the winter, and there has been a lack of sunlight.

Psychologists say this attitude is largely a result of what we focus on and talk about. If we continually talk about what is wrong, we find events and situations to support our view. However, if we talk about and focus on what is positive, our attitude can brighten. While we aren't suggesting we ignore problems and barriers that keep us from high performance, we believe that, as leaders, we need to keep hope and positive possibility alive.

Doctors know that patient health is affected by a positive attitude. Bernie Siegel, a U.S. doctor, and Norman Cousins and Candace Pert, U.S. writers, have written about the body/mind connection. Emerging research on the brain continues to show the integration of emotion and physical well-being.

U.S. educator Dave Schumaker, who has been a teacher, principal, and superintendent, has said that he asks his staff from time to time for feedback. He says, "I am not all good, and I am not all bad." If the feedback is bad, he asks his staff to give him a suggestion or two for improvement. It isn't enough just to tell him what's wrong.

We think the following story is an example of reframing or reclaiming our capacity to choose. If we talk only about what is wrong, our behaviors will follow. A positive outlook may open the doors to creative solutions and efforts.

~~~~~~~~~~~~~~~~~~~~~~

Begin by reading the story yourself. Decide whether you will use the story in your training. Make some notes about how the story does or does not fit with your work at this time. You also might want to expand on the ideas above.

_____

_____

_____

THE STORY: MY GRANDFATHER'S STORY (TWO WOLVES)

There was a grandfather. His little grandson often came in the evenings to sit at his knee and ask the many questions that children ask. One day the grandson came to his grandfather with a look of anger on his face.

Grandfather said, "Come, sit, tell me what has happened today."

The child sat and leaned his chin on his grandfather's knee. Looking up into the wrinkled, nut-brown face and the kind dark eyes, the child's anger turned to tears.

The boy said, "I went to the town today with my father – to trade the furs he has collected over the past several months. I was happy to go, because Father said that since I had helped him with the trapping, I could get something for me. Something I wanted.

"I was so excited to be in the trading post; I have not been there before. I looked at many things and finally found a metal knife! It was small … but a good size for me, so Father got it for me."

Here the boy laid his head against his grandfather's knee and became silent. The grandfather placed his hand softly on the boy's raven hair and said, "And then what happened?"

Without lifting his head, the boy said, "I went outside to wait for Father – and to admire my new knife in the sunlight. Some town boys came by and saw me, and they got all around me and started saying bad things.

"They called me dirty and stupid and said that I should not have such a fine knife. The largest of these boys pushed me back and I fell over one of the other boys. I dropped my knife, and one of them snatched it up, and they all ran away laughing."

Here the boy's anger returned. "I hate them," he said almost hoarsely. "I hate them all!"

The grandfather, with eyes that had seen too much, lifted his grandson's face so his eyes looked into the boy's. Grandfather said, "Let me tell you a story. I too have, at times, felt a great hate for those who have taken so much, with no sorrow for what they do. But hate wears you down, and it does not hurt your enemy. It is like taking poison and wishing your enemy would die. I have struggled with these feelings many times. It is as if there are two wolves inside me; one is white and one is black. The white wolf is good and does no harm. He lives in harmony with all around him and does not take offense when no offense is intended. He will fight only when it is right to do so … and in the right way.

"But the black wolf is full of anger. The littlest thing will set him off into a fit of temper. He fights everyone, all the time, for no reason. He cannot think because his anger and hate are so great. It is helpless anger, for his anger will change nothing. Sometimes it is hard to live with these two wolves inside me, for both of them try to dominate my spirit."

The boy looked into his grandfather's eyes and asked, "Which one wins, Grandfather?"

The grandfather smiled and said, "The one I feed."

QUESTIONS TO CONSIDER

1. How do you deal with your anger at work? How would you reframe that anger?

2. The story seems to reframe the nature of conflict. What are some productive or healthy ways to channel anger to resolve conflict? Describe destructive methods you've seen school staffs use to express anger and deal with conflict?

3. What cultural supports need to be in place for healthy responses to anger and conflict?

4. List and explain ways you feed the angry, fighting wolf? The harmonious wolf?

5. How do you feel hanging around people who always have something negative to say? Why?

6. How do you feel being around people who are more upbeat? Why?

WHAT IF ...

1. We helped each other feed the more productive, positive wolf?

2. We identified for one another each wolf's favorite foods?

NOTES TO MYSELF

_____

_____

_____

_____

_____

_____

_____

_____

THE TWENTY-EIGHTH FLOOR

WHY THIS STORY?

Sometimes the harder we think about a problem, the less effective we are in solving it. We have learned over the years that when an impasse occurs, it's productive to get up and do something different. Mulling over the same information and endlessly replaying the same thoughts is not a productive strategy. We have had people move to different chairs in a meeting that seemed to be going nowhere, and we've been amazed to see the results! Different thoughts or approaches emerge. Canadian professor and consultant Suzanne Bailey once told me, "Move your body, move your mind."

If you saw the movie "Dead Poets Society," you will remember that Mr. Keating (Robin Williams) had students stand on his desk to get a different perspective. Quality decisions and reflective thinking require viewing issues from multiple perspectives.

I (Bill) have a wall hanging in my office that has the *names* of colors printed in different colors. For example, the word "green" is printed in the color red. Your challenge is to say "red," the color it is printed with, instead of the word "green." After a while you probably will make a mistake and say the word that is printed; the goal, however, is to clear your mind. This helps with "split attention," and I recommend it highly for people who do a lot of presenting:
- Teachers who have to pay attention to content *and* monitor the students.
- Principals who must present information *and* monitor the faculty's emotional acceptance.

The goal of this story is to begin to talk about looking at things from different perspectives – to reframe. Given the changing landscapes, no two problems will ever be solved in the same way. Let's consider options, then choose one that has potential. If it doesn't work, let's try something else.

〰〰〰〰〰〰〰〰〰〰

Begin by reading the story yourself. Decide whether you will use the story in your training. Make some notes about how the story does or does not fit with your work at this time. You also might want to expand on the ideas above.

_____

_____

_____

_____

_____

THE STORY: THE TWENTY-EIGHTH FLOOR

Have you ever seen the world from the twenty-eighth floor? Have you ever had the chance to look out over the city and the countryside from that high point of view?

The manager of the most efficient, harmonious, and good-spirited department of a modern, international corporation was asked why the morale of his people was so high. "I take each employee on the super deluxe twenty-eighth floor tour," he responded cheerfully.

It seems that every time someone was assigned a position in his department, the manager took this person down to the basement where everything was dark and damp, covered with dust, with no natural light seeping through at all.

"How do you feel here?" the manager asked.

"Like I want to get out. It's depressing – even a bit scary."

"That's basement thinking," the manager said.

Then they went up to the lobby floor. There was always a flurry of activity, with people revolving around the doors in a hurry.

"How do you feel here?"

"Better, but confused. I don't know exactly where I'm supposed to go or what I'm supposed to do."

"That's first floor thinking."

Then the manager took the new employee up to the third floor where there was a little balcony that overlooked the street and out at the other office buildings.

"What's your reaction to this?" the manager asked pleasantly.

"I can see a little more, but it's still pretty shadowy."

"Third floor thinking."

Then they went up to the twenty-eighth floor and looked out over the whole panorama.

"How would you like a career up here?" the manager asked.

"I like it. I can see far and wide. There's light and space and room to breathe. I can see the patterns down below."

"That's thinking from the twenty-eighth floor."

"So what?" was the typical reaction.

"Close your eyes," instructed the manager. "See yourself in the basement again." The new employee went back to the basement in his mind. The manager snapped his fingers.

"Now see yourself in the lobby." The employee changed the picture on his mental movie screen. The manager snapped his fingers again. "Now see yourself on the third floor balcony." Fingers snapped. "Now see yourself on the twenty-eighth floor." The mental picture changed, and the new employee invariably smiled.

"Around here," the manager suggested, "we see all problems 'from the twenty-eighth floor.' If you ever find yourself thinking as if you were trapped in the basement, snap your fingers and go up to the twenty-eighth floor in your mind. Just snap your fingers – it's an instantaneous reminder to see from a higher point of view, and it's a call for help at the same time. If you ever snap your fingers three times in one day, come to my office. A three-snap problem is one I should know about right away!"

QUESTIONS TO CONSIDER

1. If we are building learning communities, what is the lesson of the story for us?

2. What specific behaviors are exhibited in the basement? On the first floor? How about the third floor? What about on the twenty-eighth floor? Be sure to relate some examples of behaviors commonly observed in education.

3. How do you encourage others to visit the twenty-eighth floor?

4. How can we catch ourselves earlier in the problem-solving process, so we spend more time on higher floors?

5. What are some examples of three-snap problems in education?

6. How does a problem you're working on seem to your boss? To your students? To parents? To your colleagues?

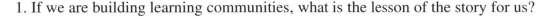

WHAT IF ...

1. We analyzed a common problem around here with basement thinking, first-floor thinking, third-floor thinking, and twenty-eighth-floor thinking?

2. I found a high place in the environment to visit when I felt I needed a twenty-eighth floor retreat? Or conversation? Or perception?

NOTES TO MYSELF

_____

_____

_____

_____

_____

_____

_____

# THE WOODEN BOWL

Why This Story?

In this story the parents make a decision about a frail old man. We were struck by the profound impact of that decision – and how hidden were its implications from the parents. It seemed so easy, so logical, so necessary to decide things in this fashion. Be conscious of what we model, as well as our efficient problem solving.

We often see the answer to a problem as easy, logical, clear. We forget the complexity and connections to other important forces. After all, we do have to do something about the spilled milk and the food on the floor.

Yet others – our collective future, really – are watching our behavior and drawing conclusions of their own. Had the adults stopped to consider the impact, they might have reconsidered their solution or fashioned something altogether different.

The story instructs us about the importance of mulling things over. Taking the time to consider the impact, consequences, or connections of our remediation is the first and often most overlooked step to a healthy solution.

Begin by reading the story yourself. Decide whether you will use the story in your training. Make some notes about how the story does or does not fit with your work at this time. You also might want to expand on the ideas above.

_____

_____

_____

_____

_____

_____

_____

THE STORY: THE WOODEN BOWL

A frail old man went to live with his son, daughter-in-law, and 4-year-old grandson. The old man's hands trembled, his eyesight was blurred, and his step faltered. The family ate together at the table, but the elderly grandfather's shaky hands and failing sight made eating difficult. Peas rolled off his spoon onto the floor. When he grasped his glass, milk spilled on the tablecloth. The son and daughter-in-law became irritated with the mess.

"We must do something about Grandfather," said the son. "I've had enough of his spilled milk, noisy eating, and food on the floor." So the husband and wife set a small table in the corner. There Grandfather ate alone while the rest of the family enjoyed dinner.

Since Grandfather had broken a dish or two, his food was served in a wooden bowl. When the family glanced in Grandfather's direction, they sometimes saw that he had a tear in his eye as he sat alone. Still, the only words the couple had for him were sharp admonitions when he dropped a fork or spilled food.

The 4-year-old watched it all in silence.

One evening before supper, the father noticed his son playing with wood scraps on the floor. He asked the child pleasantly, "What are you making?"

Just as pleasantly, the boy responded, "Oh, I am making bowls for you and Mama to eat your food when I grow up."

The 4-year-old smiled and went back to work. The words so struck the parents that they were speechless. Then tears started to stream down their cheeks. Though no word was spoken, both knew what must be done. That evening the husband took Grandfather's hand and gently led him back to the family table.

For the remainder of his days he ate every meal with the family, and neither husband nor wife seemed to care any longer when a fork was dropped, milk spilled, or the tablecloth soiled.

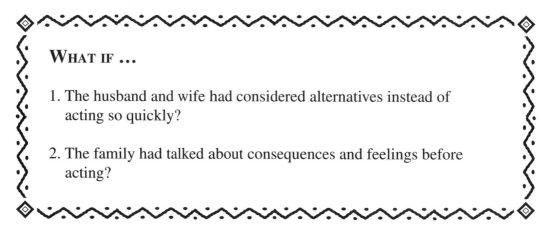

QUESTIONS TO CONSIDER

1. What do you find most important about the story? Why?

2. The solution to one problem – peas on the floor – led to a more serious and profound problem: segregating old people with difficulties as a norm that goes almost unquestioned. What solutions are you coming up with today that may be creating problems in the future? Explain.

3. What are appropriate principles by which people or groups should solve problems?

4. What do we (educators) model for students? For people new to our culture? Is that what we should be modeling? Why or why not?

5. What might be some unintended consequences of our rules and policies?

6. Are we modeling what our rules and policies state?

WHAT IF ...

1. The husband and wife had considered alternatives instead of acting so quickly?

2. The family had talked about consequences and feelings before acting?

NOTES TO MYSELF

_____

_____

_____

_____

_____

_____

FIRE AND WATER

WHY THIS STORY?

The ability to reframe is crucial to leadership. Seeing difficulties from a different perspective broadens the possibilities for solutions. Sometimes we need power. Most times we need influence.

Reflect for a minute on how true it is that a shift in perception can come from anyplace, anytime. Frequently, the shift isn't related directly to the problem or difficulty at hand. Some unrelated event or thought suddenly gives you insight into a problem with which you've struggled. Many have experienced the mundane yet serendipitous nature of this powerful epiphany.

Such is the importance of being awake – being aware, conscious, present. In this instance, an old parable from the Orient highlights a dynamic that is often hidden by the details of everyday life and choices. The story poses some questions: How do we approach our challenges? How much are we aware of the two forces named in the story? And to what extent are we capable of engineering an appropriate response to a challenge?

Clearly, our ability to see our choices and design our response will be in direct proportion to our ability to reframe relative to fire and water.

The lesson here is not only for "rulers." It is for leaders in school organizations at all levels who are passionate about creating continuously improving schools with hard work, commitment, and grace.

Begin by reading the story yourself. Decide whether you will use the story in your training. Make some notes about how the story does or does not fit with your work at this time. You also might want to expand on the ideas above.

_____

_____

_____

_____

_____

_____

The Story: Fire and Water

In the fourth century B.C., hidden within the state of Lu, lay the district over which Duke Chuang governed. The district, though small, had prospered exceedingly well under Chuang's predecessor. But since Chuang's appointment to the post, its affairs had deteriorated markedly. Taken aback by the sad turn of events, Chuang set out to the Han mountain to seek the wisdom of the great master Mu-sun.

When the duke arrived at the mountain, he found the great master sitting peacefully on a small rock looking out at the adjoining valley. After the duke had explained his situation to Mu-sun, he waited with bated breath for the great master to speak. Contrary to Chuang's expectation, however, the master whispered not a word. Rather, he smiled softly and gestured to the duke to follow him.

Silently they walked until before them lay the Tan Fu River, whose end could not be seen, it was so long and broad. After meditating on the river, Mu-sun set out to build a fire. When at last it was lit and the flames were aglow, the master had Chuang sit by his side. There they sat for hours on end as the fire burned brilliantly into the night.

With the coming of dawn, when the flames no longer danced, Mu-sun pointed to the river. Then, for the first time since the duke's arrival, the great master spoke, "Now do you understand why you are unable to do as your predecessor did – to sustain the greatness of your district?"

Chuang looked perplexed; he understood now no better than before. Slowly shame enveloped the duke. "Great master," he said, "forgive my ignorance, for the wisdom you impart I cannot comprehend." Mu-sun then spoke for the second time. "Reflect, Chuang, on the nature of the fire as it burned before us last night. It was strong and powerful. Its flames leapt upward as they danced and cried in vainglorious pride. No strong trees nor wild beasts could have matched its mighty force. With ease it could have conquered all that lay in its path.

"In contrast, Chuang, consider the river. It starts as but a small stream in the distant mountains. Sometimes it flows slowly, sometimes quickly, but always it sails downward, taking the low ground as its course. It willingly permeates every crack in the earth and willingly embraces every crevice in the land, so humble is its nature. When we listen to the water, it can scarcely be heard. When we touch it, it can scarcely be felt, so gentle is its nature.

"Yet in the end, what is left of the once mighty fire? Only a handful of ashes. For the fire is so strong, Chuang, that it not only destroys all that lies in its path but eventually falls prey to its own strength and is consumed. It is not so with the calm and quiet river. For as it was, so it is, so it will always be: forever flowing, growing deeper, broader, ever more powerful as it journeys down to the unfathomable ocean, providing life and sustenance to all."

After a moment of silence, Mu-sun turned to the duke. "As it is with nature, Chuang, so it is with rulers. For as it is not fire but water that envelops all and is the well of life, so it is not mighty and authoritative rulers but rulers with humbleness and deep-reaching inner strength who capture the people's hearts and are springs of prosperity to their states. Reflect, Chuang," continued the master, "on what type of ruler you are. Perhaps the answer that you seek will lie there."

Like a flash of lightning, the truth seized the duke's heart. No longer proud but embarrassed and uncertain, he looked up with his enlightened eye. Chuang was now blind to all but the sun rising over the river.

QUESTIONS TO CONSIDER

1. What activities are you doing that are more like fire: spectacular, bright, singular, heady?

2. What are you doing that is more water-like: humble, quiet, inclusive, detailed, flowing?

3. As you look to the future, what might you do that is fire-like? Water-like?

4. What appears to be the most important or effective approach to emphasize in your work in the future? Why?

5. Do you spend more time being fire-like or water-like? How satisfactory is the balance for you?

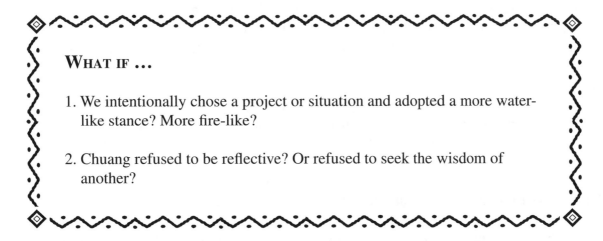

WHAT IF ...

1. We intentionally chose a project or situation and adopted a more water-like stance? More fire-like?

2. Chuang refused to be reflective? Or refused to seek the wisdom of another?

NOTES TO MYSELF

_____

_____

_____

_____

_____

_____

_____

DIVERSITY:
STRENGTHENING THE FABRIC WITH DIFFERENCES

The idea of diversity in a democratic society is a good one. It's a celebration of difference. It recognizes that different points of view make for better decisions, deeper insight. It acknowledges the importance of the whole, with many and varied parts in cooperation.

Generally, however, the idea of diversity in many organizations is quite limited. While it is an oft-stated goal, the "theory in use" is quite different from the "espoused theory," as U.S. action theorist Chris Argyris or U.S. organizational pioneer Edgar Schein might put it. Frequently, diversity means racial or ethnic diversity. Recently expanded, it might now include gender diversity. While these aspects of diversity are vitally important, they are insufficient, incomplete. Diversity's intent, its scope, is much bigger than that.

Diversity seldom means diversity with regard to thought, point of view, learning style, or values, even though it should. Because we're insensitive to the full scope of diversity, we tend to have professional "turf wars" with one another, to denigrate each other's approaches or cast doubt on the usefulness or authenticity of our colleagues' work.

What follows from this line of thinking is often a political process whereby winners and losers are created. One group musters enough strength and resources to take control of an organization, such as a board of education, curriculum, or staff development. Always there is pressure to establish and maintain a false sense of strength in unity. A "party line" becomes dominant, and all are forced to participate (or not) on that basis. "Either/or" thinking tends to elbow "both/and" thinking out of the picture.

U.S. consultant and author Peter Senge captures it exactly: "People pay a lot of lip service to diversity, but what they really don't understand is that the diversity that matters is diversity of thought. One of the reasons that diversity of background is important in any social system is because different people see the world in different ways. The problem in organizations is that usually there is a dominant worldview that suppresses all the others, and the diversity of thought that is present in the organization is lost."

The resulting culture has toxic elements. Trust, celebration of gifts and talents, and belief in our sufficiency give way to fear, mistrust, insufficiency, and alienation.

Canadian consultant and author Michael Fullan provides us with antidotes to these toxins in his writings. He advises:

◇ "Embrace diversity and resistance" (*What's Worth Fighting For in the Principalship*, p. 31).

◇ "Focus on relationships" (*What's Worth Fighting For Out There*, p. 90).

◇ "Develop and use your emotional intelligence" (*What's Worth Fighting For Out There*, p. 100).

◇ "Respect those you want to silence" (*What's Worth Fighting For Out There*, p. 111).

◇ "Move towards the danger in forming new alliances" (*What's Worth Fighting For Out There*, p. 113).

It is our hope that the stories in this section will provide an opening to talk more thoughtfully about diversity and how to be more accepting and inclusive.

RESOURCES FOR DEEPER UNDERSTANDING

♦ **ARTICLES**

Garmston, Robert. (1998). Graceful conflict: when you care enough, use the principles of effective fighting. *Journal of Staff Development*. Vol. 19, No. 3. Summer. Found at >http://www.nsdc.org/library/jsd/garmston193.html<

Hirsh, Stephanie. (2003). Resolving conflicts key to collaboration. *Results*. March. Found at >http://www.nsdc.org/library/results/res3-03hirs.html<

Richardson, Joan. (1998/1999). Common goals override individual interests. *Tools for Schools*. December/January. Found at >http://www.nsdc.org/library/tools/tools12-98rich.html<

Richardson, Joan. (2002). Listen carefully: good communication skills build relationships that foster school improvement. *Tools for Schools*. October/November. Found at >http://www.nsdc.org/library/tools/tools10-02rich.html<

♦ **THE BOOKSHELF**

Armstrong, Thomas. (1993). *Seven Kinds of Smart*. New York, NY: Plume.

Arrien, Angeles. (1993). *The Four-Fold Way: Walking Paths of the Warrior, Teacher, Healer, and Visionary.* New York, NY: HarperCollins.

Bellah, Robert N., Madsen, Richard, Sullivan, William M., Swidler, Ann, & Tipton, Steven M. (1985, 1996). *Habits of the Heart: Individualism and Commitment in American Life.* Los Angeles, CA: University of California Press.

Buckingham, Marcus, & Clifton, Donald O. (2001). *Now, Discover Your Strengths.* New York, NY: The Free Press.

Chawla, Sarita, & Renesch, John (Eds). (1995). *Learning Organizations: Developing Cultures for Tomorrow's Workplace.* Portland, OR: Productivity Press.

Fiske, Edward B. (1991). *Smart Schools, Smart Kids.* New York, NY: Touchstone.

Gilley, Kay. (1997). *Leading from the Heart.* Boston, MA: Butterworth-Heinemann.

Gray, John. (1992). *Men Are from Mars, Women Are from Venus.* New York, NY: HarperCollins.

LaBorde, Genie Z. (1983). *Influencing with Integrity.* Palo Alto, CA: Syntony Publishing.

Landsman, Julie. (2001). *A White Teacher Talks About Race.* Lanham, MD: Scarecrow Press.

Lawrence, Gordon. (1979). *People Types and Tiger Stripes.* Gainesville, FL: Center for the Application of Psychological Type.

Maybury-Lewis, David. (1992). *Millennium: Tribal Wisdom and the Modern World.* New York, NY: Viking Penguin.

Payne, Ruby K. (1995, 2003). *A Framework for Understanding Poverty* (Third Revised Edition). Highlands, TX: aha! Process.

Quinn, Daniel. (1997). *My Ishmael.* New York, NY: Bantam Books.

Seagal, Sandra, & Horne, David. (1997). *Human Dynamics.* Waltham, MA: Pegasus Communications.

We need experts, we need accurate information, but the object is not to do away with difference but to do away with muddle.
–Mary Parker Follett, U.S. author and pioneer in organizational dynamics

For everything there is a season,
And a time for every purpose under heaven:
A time to be born and a time to die,
A time to plant and a time to pluck up what is planted,
A time to kill and a time to heal,
A time to break down and a time to build up,
A time to weep and a time to laugh,
A time to mourn and a time to dance,
A time to throw away stones and a time to gather stones together,
A time to embrace and a time to refrain from embracing,
A time to seek and a time to lose,
A time to keep and a time to throw away,
A time to tear and a time to sew,
A time to keep silent and a time to speak,
A time to love and a time to hate,
A time for war and a time for peace.
–Ecclesiastes 3:1-8

Diversity: the art of thinking independently together.
–Malcolm S. Forbes, U.S. publisher

America is not a blanket woven from one thread, one color, one cloth.
–Jesse Jackson, U.S. civil rights leader and social activist

Ultimately, America's answer to the intolerant man is diversity, the very diversity which our heritage of religious freedom has inspired.
–Robert F. Kennedy, U.S. senator and attorney general

If we are to achieve a richer culture, rich in contrasting values, we must recognize the whole gamut of human potentialities, and so weave a less arbitrary social fabric, one in which each diverse human gift will find a fitting place.
–Margaret Mead, U.S. anthropologist and writer

There never were in the world two opinions alike, no more than two hairs or two grains; the most universal quality is diversity.
–Michel de Montaigne, French essayist

Abandon the urge to simplify everything, to look for formulas and easy answers, and begin to think multi-dimensionally, to glory in the mystery and paradoxes of life, not to be dismayed by the multitude of causes and consequences that are inherent in each experience – to appreciate the fact that life is complex.

–M. Scott Peck, U.S. psychiatrist and author

Toleration and liberty are the foundations of a great republic.

–Frank Lloyd Wright, U.S. architect

Honest differences are often a healthy sign of progress.

–Mahatma Gandhi, Indian philosopher and social activist

Where there is no difference, there is only indifference.

–Louis Nizer, U.S. attorney and author

If men would consider not so much where they differ as wherein they agree, there would be far less of uncharitableness and angry feeling in the world.

–Joseph Addison, British essayist

Those who are absent are always wrong.

–African proverb

Communication is a continual balancing act, juggling the conflicting needs for intimacy and independence.

–Deborah Tannen, U.S. linguistics professor and author

Be optimistic about your weaknesses; there are ways to increase your weakest intelligences, and remember: everyone has learning disabilities in something.

–Thomas Armstrong, U.S. educational consultant and author

It takes a village to raise a child.

–Nigerian proverb

One's work may be finished some day, but one's education never.

–Alexandre Dumas (the elder), French novelist and playwright

Whether you like it or not, the millions are here, and here they will remain. If you do not lift them up, they will pull you down ... Education must not simply teach work – it must teach life.

–W.E.B. Du Bois, U.S. author and civil rights leader

The function of education is to teach one to think intensively and to think critically. Intelligence plus character – that is the goal of true education.

–Martin Luther King Jr., U.S. civil rights leader and writer

The purpose of education ... is to create in a person the ability to look at the world for himself, to make his own decisions.

–James Baldwin, U.S./French writer

You can't legislate good will – that comes through education.

–Malcolm X, U.S. social activist and writer

Nothing should be overlooked in fighting for better education. Be persistent, and ornery; this will be good for the lethargic education establishment and will aid the whole cause of public education.

–Roy Wilkins, U.S. civil rights leader

Education is all a matter of building bridges.

–Ralph Ellison, U.S. essayist and novelist

I only went through 10th grade, but you'll see all kinds of textbooks around me. The more popular I become, the more I miss education. Whether you play blues or whatever, don't let people keep you like you were.

–B.B. King, U.S. blues artist

We must always go the second mile. When we go the first mile, we simply do what is required of us. It is when we go the second mile that excellence is achieved and minor miracles happen.

–Deborah McGriff, U.S. superintendent of schools

CLEANING SIDEWALKS

WHY THIS STORY?

We sometimes forget to think broadly or deeply about changes. We often think that the solution to difficulties is to tightly prescribe the answer, the response, and the process, so all are "on the same page." Habitual thinking tends to preclude sensitivity to local conditions and people's proclivity for invention and creativity.

The story "Cleaning Sidewalks" teaches us the difference between skill (doing) and being. The distinction is a difficult one in a society of human doers strongly biased toward action. Our approach seems to support the idea that if you're not doing, you're not working – as if thinking or reflecting isn't important work.

We are so busy *doing* things, forging ahead, that we forget we can't legislate or mandate what is important. While we may get results via mandates and tight schedules, we seldom get creativity and commitment. People perform minimally, constricting, hiding, avoiding one another *and* risk, engaging only when necessary.

This story is a reminder to be more patient with those who are different from us, those who have a different view of things. It's important to take the time to listen respectfully, remembering that our most important task is cultivating relationships.

It is time, we guess, to be more sensitive to diversity and inclusion as a way of understanding more deeply the challenges and complexities that face us.

Begin by reading the story yourself. Decide whether you will use the story in your training. Make some notes about how the story does or does not fit with your work at this time. You also might want to expand on the ideas above.

_____

_____

_____

_____

_____

THE STORY: CLEANING SIDEWALKS

S kill-training has its place, but what we are exploring here has less to do with skill than with something much more elusive, something that, for the point of this discussion, I'll call "being."

Skill-training has to do with "doing" – how to do this and how to do that. So let me be clear: I strongly recommend skill-training. If you are to spend time in meetings, it can be very useful to develop greater meeting skills. The same holds true for handling conflicts, dealing with difficult people, brainstorming, problem solving, and myriad other things one must do in order to survive and thrive in systems.

There are, however, many situations in which skill – how to do – is less to the point than being – how to be. Let me take a hypothetical case.

Let us say I am the youngest in the family; my brother is the oldest. Let us say that the two of us live on similar urban streets but in different cities. And let us say that both of us are troubled by – in fact, incensed over – the huge amounts of dog droppings that litter our sidewalks and sometimes find their way to the bottoms of our shoes. And let us say that both of us have spent considerable time whining and complaining about those inconsiderate dog owners who allow their pets to indiscriminately foul our sidewalks. And let us say that, coincidentally, on the same day, my brother and I separately experience epiphanies regarding the dog droppings. Suddenly, it strikes each of us separately that we have been Bottom* in the matter of dog droppings. And it strikes us that, rather than continue to be victims of this problem, we could be central to making it go away. For both of us, this is a liberating and exhilarating thought.

My brother, the first-born, has proclivities to leadership. I, the last-born, tend to do things myself. My brother organizes the neighborhood; I go out and buy a huge broom. We both succeed. He and his neighbors work out their methods; I delight in going out periodically with my broom. (Neighbors across the street mistakenly assume I was hired to do the job, so they hire their own dog-dropping technician.) Both my brother and I are delighted in our power, in our abilities to convert this complaint into an accomplishment.

Is there a skill to this? Should I learn about community organizing, or should my brother learn about broom pushing? I think not. In this, as in so many other cases, we are dealing less with doing than with being. Once the shift in being occurs, we manage to find our way to doing. On the other hand, unless there is a shift in being, all the skill-training in the world will not help.

---

* An allusion to Nick Bottom, the hilariously self-centered weaver who directs and acts in a "play within a play" in Shakespeare's *A Midsummer Night's Dream*.

QUESTIONS TO CONSIDER

1. What are some skills we need to develop (training) as educators in learning communities? Think about and describe what we get training in now.

2. What situations can you cite to support the author's idea that "there are some situations where possessing a skill is less important than knowing how to be"?
   • To what extent do you agree with his idea?
   • How important is the idea to teachers or schools?

3. As the author notes, once the shift in being occurs, we manage to find a way of doing.
   • Can you think of an example from your work life?
   • How important do you think this idea is to our work with students and each other?
   • To what extent do we practice this idea in schools?
   • How is trust related to this idea?

WHAT IF ...

1. Believers in skill-training (doing) force those who emphasize "being" into their system? And vice versa?

2. We encouraged each other to be who we are? How and why would we do that?

NOTES TO MYSELF

_____

_____

_____

_____

_____

_____

_____

THE ANIMAL SCHOOL

WHY THIS STORY?

Staff members often focus on what students can't do. Principals talk about the weaknesses of staff members. District office personnel get upset about what principals don't do. We spend a lot of precious time explaining why things aren't done like we want them, the deficiencies of others, and why no one changes. This consumes time but doesn't seem very helpful. Blame and shame have not produced creative solutions.

Yes, we would like everyone to have all the skills and knowledge that exist in the universe. The chance of that happening in our lifetime, however, is not high. Part of leadership is putting people in the right positions so they can be successful. That isn't always possible, given contracts and political situations, but it is possible more often than not.

What this story suggests to us is that sometimes we have to find out what people are good at and try to design around their strengths, not their weaknesses. Please hear this: We aren't saying we need to tolerate incompetence. We are saying that many times we have unrecognized flexibility to arrange job assignments administratively.

This story has been around for a long time. We offer it here because of its message about flexibility and talent.

Begin by reading the story yourself. Decide whether you will use the story in your training. Make some notes about how the story does or does not fit with your work at this time. You also might want to expand on the ideas above.

_____

_____

_____

_____

_____

_____

THE STORY: THE ANIMAL SCHOOL

Once upon a time, the animals decided they must do something to meet the problems of a new world, so they organized a school. They adopted an activity curriculum consisting of swimming, running, climbing, and flying. To make it easier to administer, all animals took all the subjects.

The duck was excellent in swimming, better in fact than his instructor, and made excellent grades in flying, but he was very poor in running. Since his scores were low in running, he had to stay after school and also drop swimming to practice running. The duck practiced until his webbed feet were badly worn, causing his swimming performance to drop from excellent to average. However, average was acceptable in school, so nobody worried about that except the duck.

The rabbit started at the top of the class in running, but she had a nervous breakdown from doing so much make-up work in swimming.

The squirrel was excellent in climbing until he developed frustrations in flying class, where his teacher made him start from the ground up instead of from the treetop down. He also developed charley horses from overexertion, and he got a "C" in climbing and a "D" in running.

The eagle was a problem child and had to be disciplined severely. In climbing class she beat all the others to the top of the tree but insisted on using her own way of getting there.

At the end of the year, an abnormal eel who could swim exceedingly well and also run, climb, and fly had the highest average and was valedictorian.

The prairie dogs stayed out of the school and fought the tax levy because the administration would not add digging and burrowing to the curriculum. They apprenticed their children to the badger and later joined the groundhogs and gophers to start a successful private school.

QUESTIONS TO CONSIDER

1. How does this story compare/contrast with real schools? With real classrooms? With committees?

2. To what extent is the story a description of school life for students? For staff?

3. How would you arrange the curriculum in a school? What about the issue of standards?

4. What would you say the issues are in this school?

5. What are the values of the school in the story? What are the values of the school or district where you work? Any similarities? Differences?

WHAT IF ...

1. We gave up endlessly trying to correct or shore up our deficiencies and instead chose to develop and build upon our strengths? Even our idiosyncrasies?

2. The animals decided to do something sensible instead of building a "new world" school?

NOTES TO MYSELF

_____

_____

_____

_____

_____

_____

_____

THE CRACKED POT

WHY THIS STORY?

Divergence or diversity often has unintended beneficial consequences. A friend of ours, Michael Ayers, a U.S. business and education consultant, says, "Intended consequences sometimes happen, whereas unintended consequences always happen." Apparent failure seen from a different angle can often seem to be a success. Our attitude about our endeavors is what counts most. If we get trapped into expecting perfection, we're disappointed when don't achieve it. Hence we fail to appreciate and build on our successes, even if they aren't exactly what we planned.

We're reminded of a few lines in the poem "The Prayer" by Clarissa Pinkola-Estés, a U.S. poet and writer:

> It is in the middle of misery
> that so much becomes clear.
> The one who says nothing good
> came of this,
> Is not yet listening.

Taking advantage of apparent, common flaws might lead to improvements. It's important that we know our true nature and celebrate that rather than feel bad about what we don't have or how we differ from the perceived norm.

∿∿∿∿∿∿∿∿∿∿∿

Begin by reading the story yourself. Decide whether you will use the story in your training. Make some notes about how the story does or does not fit with your work at this time. You also might want to expand on the ideas above.

_____

_____

_____

_____

_____

_____

THE STORY: THE CRACKED POT

A water bearer in India had two large pots. One pot hung on each end of a pole, which he carried across his neck. One of the pots had a crack in it, and while the other pot was perfect (and always delivered a full portion of water at the end of the long walk from the stream to the master's house), the cracked pot arrived only half full.

For two years this went on daily, with the bearer delivering only one and a half pots of water to his master's house. Of course, the perfect pot was proud of its accomplishments, perfect to the purpose for which it was made. But the poor cracked pot was ashamed of its imperfection, miserable that it was able to accomplish only half of what it had been made to do.

After two years of what it felt to be bitter failure, the cracked pot spoke to the water bearer one day by the stream. "I am ashamed of myself, and I want to apologize to you."

"Why?" asked the bearer. "What are you ashamed of?"

"I have been able, for these past two years, to deliver only half my load," the pot said, "because this crack in my side causes water to leak out all the way back to your master's house. Because of my flaw, you have to do all of this work, and you don't receive full value from your efforts."

The water bearer felt sorry for the old cracked pot and responded compassionately, "As we return to the master's house, I want you to notice the beautiful flowers along the path." Indeed, as they went up the hill, the old cracked pot took notice of the sun warming the lovely wildflowers on the side of the path, and this cheered it some. But at the end of the trail it still felt bad, because it had leaked out half its load, and so again it apologized to the bearer for its failure.

The bearer said to the pot, "Did you notice that there were flowers only on your side of your path, but not on the other pot's side? That's because I have always known about your crack, and I took advantage of it. I planted flower seeds on your side of the path, and every day while we walk back from the stream, you've watered them. For two years I've been able to pick these beautiful flowers to decorate my master's table."

"Without you being just the way you are, he would not have this beauty to grace his house."

Moral: Each of us has our own unique flaws. We're all "cracked pots." But it's the cracks and flaws we each have that make our lives together so very interesting and rewarding. (Blessed are the flexible, for they shall not be bent out of shape!) You've just got to take each person for who and what they are – and look for the good in them. There's a lot of good out there.

There's a lot of good in *you!*

QUESTIONS TO CONSIDER

1. What ideas and thoughts do you have about the story? What did you notice?

2. There is tension between perfection and imperfection in the story. The perfect pot was proud, and the imperfect pot was ashamed and miserable. How do we deal with that tension in our schools?

3. How do we get agreement about expectations in a community of learners? Are they too low, too high, or just about right?

4. How are "cracked pots" treated in schools? Are they seen as "crackpots," or are they validated for the worth they have? How do "perfect pots" tend to be treated in schools?

5. Cite some examples from your own settings to illustrate the point of the story.

6. One theme of the story relates to diversity. How diverse are we as a community or a school? What do you mean by diversity?

7. There's also a theme of unintended (unplanned) consequences. See if you can think of unintended consequences (positive or negative) related to schools.

WHAT IF ...

1. The water bearer had fixed the cracked pot (or we attempt to fix "cracked pots" in our schools)?

2. The water bearer wasn't compassionate and hadn't planted the flowers?

NOTES TO MYSELF

_____

_____

_____

_____

_____

◈ TWO HAWKS ◈

WHY THIS STORY?

Many times in schools we focus on difference as a source of tension. U.S. Pulitzer Prize-winning author Edward O. Wilson, in a book called *Diversity of Life,* said, "Diversity strengthens," but we don't believe most people or organizations exemplify this very well. Think of the last time you were on an interview team. As you may have observed, we educators tend to hire people who are like us, rather than hire for differences or for skills we don't have.

When I (Bill) first came to Minneapolis in 1970, the city's elms were suffering from Dutch elm disease. Many trees were lost, and the city looked barren in some areas. Fortunately, the city founders had planted a wide variety of trees. If the only trees planted had been elm trees, the city would have looked much worse than it did. Of course, 35 years later, new trees have flourished, and Minneapolis has a different feel.

This story shows that our perceived disabilities can be our strengths. Sometimes we must reframe an experience or skill to see the potential of our weaknesses to work in our favor. Context often determines which strengths are needed.

∿∿∿∿∿∿∿∿∿∿∿

Begin by reading the story yourself. Decide whether you will use the story in your training. Make some notes about how the story does or does not fit with your work at this time. You also might want to expand on the ideas above.

_____

_____

_____

_____

_____

_____

_____

_____

THE STORY: TWO HAWKS

There are two hawks that live in an open area. One hawk has excellent eyesight and can see what animals are on the ground from hundreds of feet in the air. This hawk really likes frogs. Since he can see well, he waits until he sees one, then dives down to get the frog and eats it.

The other hawk has poor eyesight. The hawk can see movement but can't really tell what kind of animal is on the ground. When this hawk dives it may get a frog, a lizard, field mouse, etc. It is happy to get food, period.

One day the environment changes, and the frog population is affected. The number of frogs decreases. Which hawk will survive better in this changing environment?

QUESTIONS TO CONSIDER

1. Under what conditions may a perceived weakness become a strength in individuals or groups?

2. When might our strengths become weaknesses for our organization? A U.S. marriage counselor once said, "Strengths overextended can become weaknesses." What do you think of that statement?

3. How do we incorporate differences into the leadership and operations of our school?

4. How do we foster appreciation for diversity in our organization?

5. How do you compensate for your weaknesses?

WHAT IF ...

1. We saw our limitations as potential strengths?

2. We found the strengths in our students, instead of their deficits?

NOTES TO MYSELF

_____

_____

_____

_____

_____

_____

_____

_____

_____

_____

 THE GABRA

Why This Story?

Indigenous cultures have survived for thousands of years. At times governments or helping agencies try to help these cultures. Sometimes the help is not helpful. Understanding cultures and the interdependence of the people in those cultures must come first, before one tries to develop programs to assist.

The story of the Gabra depicts the relationship of the people who live in Kenya's Chalbi Desert to the desert itself. In their years of living there, the Gabra developed traditions that the government needed to understand before it implemented plans thought to be helpful.

This process happens in school communities as well. A program is developed, sometimes without much input from the people in the community. Many times important relationships, cultural norms, and ways of doing things are inadvertently excluded, though they would be beneficial to the process of change. Anyone trying to provide assistance needs to know the culture before trying to change the culture. Help is only help if it is seen and received as help.

Begin by reading the story yourself. Decide whether you will use the story in your training. Make some notes about how the story does or does not fit with your work at this time. You also might want to expand on the ideas above.

_____

_____

_____

_____

_____

_____

_____

_____

THE STORY: THE GABRA

One of the few remaining nomadic peoples of East Africa is the Gabra, who live in northern Kenya. A space traveler who touched down in Gabra country might wonder if he or she had landed on the wrong planet, for the trackless red expanses of the Chalbi Desert seem more like Mars than our own green earth. But the Gabra consider this wilderness their land, and they see it as a place of freedom and fertility. There is water for those who know where to look, good grasses and bad grasses, and protective trees standing like shrines under the sheltering sky. Above all, it is a good land for camels, and it is camels that define the Gabra.

The nomadic Gabra also keep cattle and goats, but they may be tended by herders as far away as 200 miles from the community. The Gabra camp travels with the camels, the animals meandering through and around the Chalbi Desert, constantly moving in search of forage or to get away from their own dung. Aversion to dung is not just a whim on the part of these notoriously whimsical beasts, as ticks collect in the dung and make the camels' lives miserable. They may do even worse than that, for the ticks sometimes carry a disease that can be fatal to camels. So the camels must move – and the people with them.

If possible, the Gabra pick a new site that can be reached in a day, in order to avoid spending a night in the open with their huts and all their possessions loaded on their camels. The Gabra aren't averse, though, to moving 50 miles or more when necessary. Every eight years or so they make long pilgrimages to their sacred sites in southern Ethiopia, where Gabra men go through ceremonies that enable them to graduate from one age-set to the next. On these journeys the community must build thorn fences for their smaller animals, while the camels, the cattle, and the Gabra themselves sleep in the open under the enveloping skies.

But there is drama even in routine migrations. People become restless once the decision to move on has been made, and women often get up in the middle of the night to begin dismantling their household. If there is no moon, they have to do this by touch in the darkness, which is possible because everything in the household has a specific place and is packed and loaded in a certain order. The men tie upright poles onto the camels, and the women roll up everything in the household – even the outer skins of the huts themselves – and pack it all between the poles. The poles are then bound together and lashed tightly by ropes onto the camels. All of the packing and loading is done by women. Men take no part in it other than to restrain the camels if they become unruly or to help lift items that are too heavy for the women.

The Gabra live their entire lives in these unending cycles of migration. The movement is necessary in order to live off their land, but the Gabra still love their desert and see it as a supportive environment where they can live with dignity. They know how to use their land and to conserve its resources. They move even before they're forced so as to ensure that the land is replenished for the future. When the rains come, they leave their dry-season pastures and move up into the highlands. They could stay in the lowlands, but then the area would be overgrazed when the dry season came round again.

They manage their pasturelands by setting controlled fires to drive back the bush. Because their herds soon denude an area of edible grasses, leaving only unpalatable ones, the Gabra burn off the bad grasses to allow the good ones to flourish in the ash. They are also careful of trees. Full-grown acacia trees are protected, for example, and called "bulls," for they regenerate the landscape just as bulls regenerate the herd; trees of another kind, whose supple branches make them particularly useful, and whose spreading roots stabilize underground water sources, are considered sacred and treated as shrines.

This sense of the sacred permeates the Gabra landscape and protects it. Aneesa Kassam, who studies the Gabra, writes that their philosophy of life can be summed up in their idea of "finn," meaning fertility and plenty. The sky god sends rain to bless the earth, make the grass grow, and ensure that animals and humans have enough to eat and can grow fat. Finn is the earth and the cycle of life that takes place upon it. Human beings contribute to finn as they care for the earth and for their animals, as they exchange livestock, nourish friendships, exchange ideas, tell tales, or sing songs. They and their wanderings are part of a constant cycle of creation and replenishment.

Not long ago the Gabra briefly became the victims of well-intentioned "experts." While Kenya was still a British colony, the authorities decided to prohibit the Gabra from firing their grasslands in the old-fashioned way. The prohibition resulted in a buildup of deadwood that caused a huge fire, which raged out of control and destroyed a large part of the forest on Marsabit Mountain. Since then, the Gabra's own small and controlled fires have been looked upon as a useful and intelligent practice. Nowadays Kenyan ranches are using the Gabra combination of camel browsing and range firing to keep the grasslands under control.

In part because of vindications like this one, the Kenyan government has begun to realize that taking the nomads off the land is not necessarily a wise thing to do and may, in fact, contribute to ecological degradation. It has become clear that, if the deserts of Africa are spreading, it isn't because of the nomads and their way of life – for their survival has always depended on cultivating a harmonious relationship with their environment. The fault is more likely to lie in efforts to squeeze the economic contributions that governments have a "right" to expect out of regions that have traditionally been used by nomadic herders. Such is the legacy of Western-style development thinking. It often is disastrous for indigenous peoples because planners neglect or scorn their knowledge, thereby belittling one of humankind's greatest attributes – adaptability. Humans can live almost anywhere, given ecological knowledge and the appropriate social relations.

The best development planning takes into account both the interests and the expertise of those in the areas to be "developed." Where this is done, indigenous peoples do not suffer needlessly from a "development" in which they have had no say.

QUESTIONS TO CONSIDER:

1. How is your community like the Gabra? Unlike the Gabra?

2. Has there been a time when outside forces have tried to implement a program or a way to help your organization that did not work out? What happened? What would have made the outside contribution work?

3. What can we learn from the story of the Gabra that is applicable to our organization?

4. What other stories have you read that have a similar theme?

5. What recommendations, if any, would you make to your organization based on the story of the Gabra?

WHAT IF ...

1. We listened to students to provide some guidance in policy formation?

2. We saw children from poverty as everyone's responsibility?

NOTES TO MYSELF

_____

_____

_____

_____

_____

_____

_____

CONFLICT: CREATIVELY USING NATURAL ENERGY

We don't know anyone who lives a conflict-free life. In education especially, conflict takes lots of energy and resources. Do you think conflict will increase, decrease, or stay the same? We have asked that question to groups over the past three years, and not one has predicted that conflict will decrease.

If conflict is not decreasing, the only option is to learn more strategies to deal with conflict constructively. As a matter of fact, we may not even *want* conflict-free situations. Creativity comes from conflict between what is and what could be; this is called creative tension. Conflict occurs as people plan alternative futures and deal with knotty problems. The trick is to manage conflict in schools in order to get positive results from conflict and not derail good people and good thinking.

U.S. business professor Allen C. Amason and his colleagues write about "A" conflict and "C" conflict. "A" conflict is affective (not to be confused with effective) conflict, which can be very destructive to individuals, schools, and districts. Examples of affective conflict would be "Who does he think he is?" or "She thinks she's so smart." On the other hand, "C" conflict, where people can talk about their beliefs and the differences in those beliefs, can be a catalyst for more creativity, increasing trust, and improving teamwork. Those "C" characteristics are elements of productive organizations and learning communities.

Each of the compilers of this collection of stories has been in more conflict situations than he wanted to. However, our combined experience tells us the value of being able to manage conflict for positive outcomes. The point we would like to emphasize is that the pre-eminent need is to first manage conflict internally – not internally within our organizations but internally within ourselves! U.S. entrepreneur Dee Hock, founder of VISA International and Terre Civitas, says we should spend 40% of our time managing ourselves by paying attention to our own responses to conflict.

With continued stress on testing, standards, and improvement in schools, there will be no shortage of pressure and, therefore, conflict situations. We hope these stories will enable you to provide ways of starting the conversation about how to deal openly and positively with conflict.

RESOURCES FOR DEEPER UNDERSTANDING

◆ ARTICLES

NSDC (National Staff Development Council) Library: Conflict Resolution at: >http://nsdc.org/educatorindex.htm<

Garmston, Robert. (1998). Graceful conflict: when you care enough, use the principles of effective fighting. *Journal of Staff Development.* Vol. 19, No. 3. Summer. Found at >http://www.nsdc.org/library/jsd/garmston193.html<

Killion, Joellen. (1998). Learning depends on teacher knowledge. *Results.* December.

Richardson, Joan. (1998/1999). Common goals override individual interests. *Tools for Schools.* December/January.

Sparks, Dennis. (2002). Improved social relationships are fundamental. *Results.* February. Found at >http://www.nsdc.org/library/results/res2-02spar.html<

◆ THE BOOKSHELF

Block, Peter. (1987). *The Empowered Manager.* San Francisco, CA: Jossey-Bass.

Brinkman, Rick, & Kirschner, Rick. (1994). *Dealing with People You Can't Stand.* Chicago, IL: R.R. Donnelley & Sons.

Carse, James P. (1986). *Finite and Infinite Games.* New York, NY: Ballantine Books.

Crum, Thomas F. (1987). *The Magic of Conflict.* New York, NY: Touchstone.

Fisher, Roger, & Brown, Scott. (1988). *Getting Together.* New York, NY: Penguin Books.

Fisher, Roger, & Ury, William. (1981). *Getting to YES.* New York, NY: Penguin Books.

Tzu, Sun. (1963). *The Art of War* (translated by Samuel B. Griffith). Oxford, England: Oxford University Press.

Ury, William. (1991). *Getting Past NO.* New York, NY: Bantam Books.

Conflict in and of itself is not a negative experience ... It is how we choose to respond to conflict that determines whether its effect will be positive or negative ... Instead of believing that we know all the answers, we embrace curiosity.
–The Tao of Negotiation (Joel Edelman and Mary Beth Crain, U.S. writers)

Conflict itself is, of course, a sign of health, as you would know if you ever met really apathetic people, really hopeless people, people who have given up hoping, striving, coping.
–Abraham Maslow, U.S. psychoanalyst and author

Every fight is on some level a fight between differing "angles of vision" illuminating the same truth.
–Mahatma Gandhi, Indian philosopher and social activist

[O]ne person's decision to respond rather than react to that situation ... can set the stage for dialogue and openness.
–The Tao of Negotiation (Joel Edelman and Mary Beth Crain)

Embrace conflict for the creative tension. Think of conflict as positive interaction for the discovery of creative solutions.
–Great Lakes Area Regional Resource Center (U.S.)

Have you learned lessons only of those who admired you, and were tender with you, and stood aside for you? Have you not learned great lessons from those who braced themselves against you, and disputed the passage with you?
–Walt Whitman, U.S. poet

These basic human needs are ... at the heart of every conflict ... We all want to be appreciated, respected, acknowledged.
–The Tao of Negotiation (Joel Edelman and Mary Beth Crain)

The world will be regenerated by the people who ... heroically seek ... by whatever hardship, by whatever toil, the methods by which people can agree.
–Mary Parker Follett, U.S. author and pioneer in organizational dynamics

Difference of opinion leads to inquiry, and inquiry to truth.
–Thomas Jefferson, third U.S. president

If you have an important point to make, don't try to be subtle or clever. Use a pile driver. Hit the point once. Then come back and hit it again. Then hit it a third time – a tremendous whack.
–Winston Churchill, British prime minister

It is easier to stay out than get out.
–Chinese proverb

# EPILOGUE: A SOFT ANSWER

WHY THIS STORY?

Conflict is an inevitable part of working together in schools. How we handle it is a matter of crucial importance. Do we see it as a threat, or is it an opportunity for growth? Do we shut down and get defensive, or can we learn other ways to practice listening and exploring?

This story instructs us that often there are overlooked dimensions to conflicts. It reminds us that perhaps the best advice is not to exacerbate the situation. The considerable energy of a situation can sometimes be used for resolution, understanding, and progress. Force, physical strength, and verbal facility aren't necessarily what a situation requires. Power usually gets a power response. This happens in conflictual situations between nations, and it happens between individuals and groups. Clearly, it's in our collective interest to have a kit bag full of attitudes, strategies, and awarenesses to apply in different situations – a diverse approach.

While we observe the wisdom of the improvising old man, we also notice the sensitivity of the young man as he patiently lets the situation unfold, untethered from the compulsion to act, yet ready to participate. Managing conflicts successfully requires creativity.

Finally, there is an element of surprise. A human being acts surprisingly kind and gentle in a situation that seems to call for defensiveness, protection, and strength. Staying loose and flexible keeps us open to exploiting opportunities to create healthier outcomes.

〰〰〰〰〰〰〰〰

Begin by reading the story yourself. Decide whether you will use the story in your training. Make some notes about how the story does or does not fit with your work at this time. You also might want to expand on the ideas above.

_____

_____

_____

_____

_____

_____

THE STORY: EPILOGUE: A SOFT ANSWER

A turning point in my life came one day on a train in the suburbs of Tokyo in the middle of a drowsy spring afternoon. The old car clanking and rattling over the rails was comparatively empty – a few housewives with their kids in tow, some old folks out shopping, a couple of off-duty bartenders studying the racing form. I gazed absently at the drab houses and dusty hedgerows.

At one station the doors opened and suddenly the quiet afternoon was shattered by a man bellowing at the top of his lungs, yelling violent, obscene, incomprehensible curses. Just as the doors closed, the man, still yelling, staggered into our car. He was big, drunk, and dirty, dressed in laborer's clothing. His bulging eyes were demonic, neon red. His hair was crusted with filth. Screaming, he swung at the first person he saw, a woman holding a baby. The blow glanced off her shoulder, sending her spinning into the laps of an elderly couple. It was a miracle that the baby was unharmed.

The terrified couple jumped up and scrambled toward the other end of the car. The laborer aimed a kick at the retreating back of the old lady, but he missed and she scuttled to safety. This so enraged the drunk that he grabbed the metal pole in the center of the car and tried to wrench it out of its stanchion. I could see that one of his hands was cut and bleeding. The train lurched ahead, the passengers frozen with fear.

I stood up. At the time, I was young, in pretty good shape, was six feet tall, and weighed 225 pounds. I'd been putting in a solid eight hours of Aikido training every day for the past three years and I thought I was tough. The trouble was, my martial skill was untested in actual combat. As a student of Aikido, I was not allowed to fight.

My teacher, the founder of Aikido, taught us each morning that the art was devoted to peace. "Aikido," he said again and again, "is the art of reconciliation. Whoever has the mind to fight has broken his connection with the universe. If you try to dominate other people, you are already defeated. We study how to resolve conflict, not how to start it."

I listened to his words. I tried hard. I wanted to quit fighting. I had even gone so far as to cross the street a few times to avoid the *chimpira,* the pinball punks who lounged around the train stations. They'd have been happy to test my martial ability. My forbearance exalted me. I felt both tough and holy. In my heart of hearts, however, I was dying to be a hero. I wanted a chance, an absolutely legitimate opportunity whereby I might save the innocent by destroying the guilty.

"This is it!" I said to myself as I got to my feet. "This slob, this animal, is drunk and mean and violent. People are in danger. If I don't do something fast, somebody will probably get hurt."

Seeing me stand up, the drunk recognized a chance to focus his rage. "Aha!" he roared. "A foreigner! You need a lesson in Japanese manners!" He punches the metal pole once to give weight to his words.

Hanging on lightly to the commuter strap overhead, I gave him a slow look of disgust and dismissal – every bit of nastiness I could summon up. I planned to take this turkey apart, but he had to be the one to move first. And I wanted him mad, because the madder he got, the more certain my victory. I pursed my lips and blew him a sneering, insolent kiss that hit him like a slap in the face. "All right!" he hollered. "You're gonna get a lesson." He gathered himself for a rush at me. He would never know what hit him.

A split second before he moved, someone shouted "Hey!" It was ear-splitting. I remember being struck by the strangely joyous, lilting quality of it, as though you and a friend had been searching diligently for something and had suddenly stumbled upon it. "Hey!"

I wheeled to my left, the drunk spun to his right. We both stared down at a little old Japanese man. He must have been well into his seventies. He took no notice of me but beamed delightedly at the laborer, as though he had a most important, most welcome secret to share.

"C'mere," the old man said in an easy vernacular, beckoning to the drunk. "C'mere and talk with me." He waved his hand lightly. The big man followed, as if on a string. He planted his feet belligerently in front of the old gentleman, towering threateningly over him. "Talk to you," he roared above the clacking wheels. "Why the hell should I talk to you?"

The old man continued to beam at the laborer. There was not a trace of fear or resentment about him. "What'cha been drinking?" he asked lightly, his eyes sparkling with interest.

"I been drinkin' sake," the laborer bellowed back, "and it's none of your goddam business!" Flecks of spittle spattered the old man.

"Oh, that's wonderful," the old man said with delight. "Absolutely wonderful! You see, I love sake, too. Every night, me and my wife (she's seventy-six, you know), we warm up a little bottle of sake and take it out into the garden, and we sit on the old wooden bench that my grandfather's first student made for him. We watch the sun go down, and we look to see how our persimmon tree is doing. My great-grandfather planted that tree, and we worry about whether it will recover from those ice storms we had last winter. Persimmons do not do well after ice storms, although I must say that ours has done rather better than I expected, especially when you consider the poor quality of the soil. Still, it is most gratifying to watch when we take our sake and go out to enjoy the evening – even when it rains!" He looked up at the laborer, eyes twinkling, happy to share his delightful information.

As he struggled to follow the intricacies of the old man's conversation, the drunk's face began to soften. His fists slowly unclenched. "Yeah," he said slowly, "I love persimmons, too ..." His voice trailed off.

"Yes," said the old man, smiling, "and I'm sure you have a wonderful wife."

"No," replied the laborer. "My wife died." He hung his head. Very gently, swaying with the motion of the train, the big man began to sob. "I don't got no wife. I don't got no home. I don't got no job. I don't got no money. I don't got nowhere to go." Tears rolled down his cheeks, and a spasm of pure despair rippled through his body. Above the baggage rack a four-color ad trumpeted the virtues of suburban luxury living.

Now it was my turn. Standing there in my well-scrubbed youthful innocence, my make-this-world-safe-for-democracy righteousness, I suddenly felt dirtier than the drunk was.

Just then the train arrived at my stop. The platform was packed, and the crowd surged into the car as soon the doors opened. Maneuvering my way out, I heard the old man cluck sympathetically. "My, my," he said with undiminished delight. "That is a very difficult predicament, indeed. Sit down here and tell me about it."

I turned my head for one last look. The laborer was sprawled like a sack on the seat, his head in the old man's lap. The old man looked down at him, all compassion and delight, one hand softly stroking the filthy, matted head.

As the train pulled away, I sat down on a bench. What I had wanted to do with muscle and meanness had been accomplished with kind words. I had seen Aikido tried in combat, and the essence of it was love, as the founder had said. I would have to practice the art with an entirely different spirit. It would be a long time before I could speak about the resolution of conflict.

Questions to Consider

1. When we are building learning communities, what are the lessons from this story that we would do well to keep in mind?

2. How is conflict dealt with in the story? What are the implications for us in dealing with conflict in our own environment?

3. What attitudes do you see in the story that got in the way of dealing with the central problem? What attitudes get in the way of solving our problems?

4. The author says, "I would have to practice the art with an entirely different spirit." What practices around here require "an entirely different spirit"?

5. Are most of your conflicts "A"-type or "C"-type? Explain.

6. How do you prepare when you have a difficult conversation to attend to?

What if ...

1. The narrator hadn't waited and took on the drunk straightaway?

2. The old man kept to himself?

Notes to Myself

_____

_____

_____

_____

_____

_____

_____

THE WIND AND THE SUN

WHY THIS STORY?

When in conflict, we sometimes respond first with more power. Think of a time a colleague, student, or parent came to you and accused you of something or attacked you. Did you remain calm, or was your first inclination to get mad, to protect yourself, and to counterattack?

Our brains are wired to respond emotionally first. By the time we reach adulthood, most of us have developed ways to be less impulsive, to think before we act. Students – and some adults – have not learned these techniques very well, or they've forgotten, or they're out of practice.

This story is an example of how to deal with conflicts in more than one way. Force, power, anger, and impulsivity are all ways to deal with problems, but often we must seek other solutions. As a matter of fact, sometimes power, force, and anger will make the problems worse.

Another reason we value this story is that we, as adults, must model what we want for kids. You can't give what you don't have. Students are watching adults all the time. They may not tell us that; they may even act like they are ignoring us. But, rest assured, they watch us constantly. If we don't model appropriate behavior, children and teenagers will not have models to emulate.

Begin by reading the story yourself. Decide whether you will use the story in your training. Make some notes about how the story does or does not fit with your work at this time. You also might want to expand on the ideas above.

_____

_____

_____

_____

_____

_____

_____

_____

THE STORY: THE WIND AND THE SUN

The wind and the sun, both gifted and powerful in their own ways, began to argue like children about who was the strongest.

The wind boasted of its awesome power to bend trees, strip leaves from branches, and hurl hurricanes and tornadoes at the land.

The sun boasted of its ability to melt snow, warm the earth, make flowers bloom, and create wonderful golden days.

As they argued, it became clear that they should have a contest. They spied a man down below walking on a road. Which one could make the oblivious traveler take off his coat?

The wind blew ferociously. Dark clouds hid the sun, and the air was filled with leaves and dust. The air roiled with energy. Chilled, the tired traveler gripped his coat more tightly and buried his face deeper.

The wind grew weary and relinquished his turn to the sun. The sun smiled, seizing the opportunity. As the sun beamed brighter, the traveler loosened his grip on his coat. He raised his head and breathed more easily at the warmth. Finally, the traveler became so warm that he took off his coat, sat down by a stream, and had a cool drink of water before continuing his journey.

 **QUESTIONS TO CONSIDER**

1. What does this story about the wind and the sun have to do with managing conflict or advancing one's program or agenda?

2. What behaviors and attitudes are "sun"? Which are "wind"? How do they influence the culture of the school (organization)?

3. The contest in this story might be seen as absurd or childish. A great deal of energy is expended by both parties as they try to prove a hubristic point. What examples can you cite in your school culture or organization similar to this?

4. What conflicts seem to be settled by acting like the sun? How did you know?

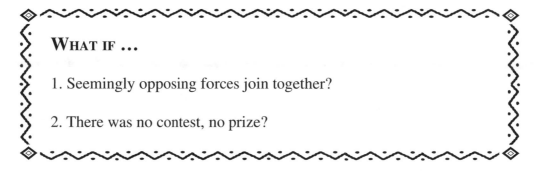

WHAT IF ...

1. Seemingly opposing forces join together?

2. There was no contest, no prize?

NOTES TO MYSELF

_____

_____

_____

_____

_____

_____

_____

_____

_____

_____

THE WISDOM OF THE MOUNTAIN

WHY THIS STORY?

How much of a conflict can be attributed to the inability to see another's reality? One of the lessons of this story is that what you can't see from one part of the mountain may be perfectly visible from another part. Conflict resolution is sometimes a matter of coming down from atop a mountain of assumptions and inferences to examine your own and others' firmly held beliefs.

Seeing from different perspectives widens our sense of reality. There are always multiple realities, depending upon where you sit. Think of a breakfast of ham and eggs. The chicken makes a mere contribution, while for the pig it's a full commitment!

"The Wisdom of the Mountain" reminds us of the importance of quietly being aware of other realities, thus opening the door to deeper understanding and less conflict. An Estonian proverb says, "Silence is sometimes the answer." Most reflection begins by being quiet, taking deep breaths, and focusing thoughts on multiple viewpoints. U.S. novelist F. Scott Fitzgerald once said that intelligence is being able to hold two opposing ideas in your mind at the same time and still retain the ability to function.

Awareness of multiple points of view is only the beginning. Though significant, simple awareness has to be followed up with genuine inquiry into all the dimensions of another point of view. After all, the object is to fully and completely understand multiple points of view.

~~~~~~~~~~~~~~~~~~~~

Begin by reading the story yourself. Decide whether you will use the story in your training. Make some notes about how the story does or does not fit with your work at this time. You also might want to expand on the ideas above.

_____

_____

_____

_____

_____

_____

THE STORY: THE WISDOM OF THE MOUNTAIN

In ancient China, on top of Mount Ping stood a temple where the enlightened one, Hwan, dwelled. Of his many disciples, only one is known to us, Lao-li. For more than 20 years, Lao-li studied and meditated under the great master, Hwan. Although Lao-li was one of the brightest and most determined of disciples, he had yet to reach enlightenment. The wisdom of life was not his.

Lao-li struggled with his lot for days, nights, months, even years until one morning, the sight of a falling cherry blossom spoke to his heart. "I can no longer fight my destiny," he reflected. "Like the cherry blossom, I must gracefully resign myself to my lot." From that moment forth, Lao-Li determined to retreat down the mountain, giving up his hope of enlightenment.

Lao-li searched for Hwan to tell him of his decision. The master sat before a white wall, deep in meditation. Reverently, Lao-li approached him. "Enlightened one," he said. But before he could continue, the master spoke, "Tomorrow I will join you on your journey down the mountain." No more needed to be said. The great master understood.

The next morning, before their descent, the master looked out into the vastness surrounding the mountain peak. "Tell me, Lao-li," he said, "what do you see?" "Master, I see the sun beginning to wake just below the horizon, meandering hills and mountains that go on for miles, and couched in the valley below, a lake and an old town." The master listened to Lao-li's response. He smiled, and then they took the first steps of their long descent.

Hour after hour, as the sun crossed the sky, they pursued their journey, stopping only once as they approached the foot of the mountain. Again Hwan asked Lao-li to tell him what he saw. "Great wise one, in the distance I see roosters as they run around barns, cows asleep in sprouting meadows, old ones basking in the late afternoon sun, and children romping by a brook." The master, remaining silent, continued to walk until they reached the gate to the town. There the master gestured to Lao-li, and together they sat under an old tree. "What did you learn today, Lao-li?" asked the master. "Perhaps this is the last wisdom I will impart to you." Silence was Lao-li's response.

At last, after long silence, the master continued. "The road to enlightenment is like the journey down the mountain. It comes only to those who realize that what one sees at the top of the mountain is not what one sees at the bottom. Without this wisdom, we close our minds to all that we cannot view from our position and so limit our capacity to grow and improve. But with this wisdom, Lao-li, there comes an awakening. We recognize that alone one sees only so much – which, in truth, is not much at all. This is the wisdom that opens our minds to improvement, knocks down prejudices, and teaches us to respect what at first we cannot view. Never forget this last lesson, Lao-li: what you cannot see can be seen from a different part of the mountain."

When the master stopped speaking, Lao-li looked out to the horizon, and as the sun set before him, it seemed to rise in his heart. Lao-li turned to the master, but the great one was gone. So the old Chinese tale ends. But it has been said that Lao-li returned to the mountain to live out his life. He became a great enlightened one.

QUESTIONS TO CONSIDER

1. What lessons or what wisdom do you take from the story?

2. How important is this wisdom to our work in the field of education?

3. There seems to be another important lesson exemplified in Lao-li's pursuit of wisdom all those years. Just at the time of giving up, the needed lesson arrived from an unlikely place and made all the difference to him. To what extent are we disciplined in our work to *keep at* something we value?

4. How can the process of giving up open new possibilities?

5. How do we manage the tension between disciplined practice and the pressures to give up, to abandon our efforts? Are we in balance?

6. Are there appropriate times to give up or give in? When? Should we consider giving up on some things? An expression from Christendom, "Let go and let God," speaks to the search for balance between our own efforts and simply receiving wisdom.

7. Where are you making "contributions"? Where are you demonstrating "full commitment"?

WHAT IF ...

1. Lao-li had not surrendered to his fate?

2. Lao-li had not tried so hard all those years to be enlightened?

NOTES TO MYSELF

_____

_____

_____

_____

_____

GETTING WHAT YOU WANT – THE OTHER WAY

WHY THIS STORY?

Conflict frequently causes us to constrict, triggering an inability to remain flexible, open, and breathing. Conflict frequently takes on a fight-or-flight cast, provokes a win/lose mentality, and prompts feelings of being threatened, all of which cause us to react defensively. We also tend to react rashly, without considering healthy alternatives. We lose our objectivity, our ability to observe as witnesses. Instead, we tend to react immediately as participants.

The old man in this story demonstrates to us the importance of flexibility in dealing with difficulties. The story cues us to remember our response-ability – our personal power to influence the outcome of circumstances. The story also reminds us of the importance of play, humor, and the counterintuitive in the midst of our difficulties. Sometimes the best answer comes from the oddest of places.

Begin by reading the story yourself. Decide whether you will use the story in your training. Make some notes about how the story does or does not fit with your work at this time. You also might want to expand on the ideas above.

_____

_____

_____

_____

_____

_____

_____

_____

THE STORY: GETTING WHAT YOU WANT – THE OTHER WAY

There is a story of an elderly man who lived in a house on a corner. His corner lot had a fence around it. The house was on the way to an elementary school. It seemed like every day kids would come by and throw paper wrappers, pop cans, or schoolwork in his yard.

The man thought about confronting the young lads but didn't want to yell at them, as he didn't want them to be even more inconsiderate. One day he caught the boys going by his house. He said, "I know you are throwing stuff over the fence into my yard." The boys immediately denied they had ever done that.

The man continued, "I have seen you do it." The boys were about to run when the man said, "Wait a minute, I want you to throw stuff on my lawn." The young boys were puzzled. They thought he was crazy. The man said, "To show you I'm serious, I will give you one dollar for every day you throw your garbage into my yard." Now the boys knew the old man was crazy, but they said they would do it.

The next day the boys tested the man. They threw papers over the fence. The man waited by the side of the house, came out, and gave them a dollar. He told them they did a good job and to keep doing it. This went on for two weeks.

After two weeks the man met the young boys and said, "This is getting expensive, and I can't afford to pay you a dollar a day. I'll give you a quarter a day if you keep throwing your papers over the fence."

The boys responded, "Who do you think we are? We aren't going to do this for a quarter!" The man never had to clean up his yard again.

Questions to Consider

1. How do people normally react in a situation like this one? What, generally, are the results in such situations?

2. In the story, the man weighs his alternatives. Confrontation would have meant yelling and more inconsiderate behavior by the boys. So he sought an alternative. What is required of people in order for them to stop, think, and seek another alternative? Explain a situation you've seen in your setting where slowing down and exploring alternatives would certainly have been better.

3. What skills and attitudes are required to "shape-shift" a circumstance from one that was potentially destructive to one that is potentially constructive? And why bother with constructive at all?

4. Are there examples from your workplace where motivation and rewards might be changed to make the outcomes of difficulties more positive? What changes can you personally make? Explain.

What If ...

1. The man got angry, yelled, or called the police?

2. The kids simply refused to talk to the elderly man?

Notes to Myself

_____

_____

_____

_____

_____

_____

_____

_____

# THE ORANGE AND THE SISTERS

WHY THIS STORY?

Conflict happens internally and externally. Scarcity usually results in conflict. Think about when budget or staffing numbers are released to a school. Departments compete for money and people. This is a classic "fixed pie" or "tragedy of the commons" system being played out.

When we focus on what we want, sometimes we lose sight of what others want. It may be that we jump to conclusions about what is important. We might make the assumption that others want the same things we do. This is why dialogue is so important, especially in times of scarcity.

In the following story, a conflict arises between two sisters and is resolved; however, had outcomes been discussed before the manner of resolution was decided, the resolution may have been more satisfying to each sister. This story exemplifies the reason we talk first before getting into confrontations.

Begin by reading the story yourself. Decide whether you will use the story in your training. Make some notes about how the story does or does not fit with your work at this time. You also might want to expand on the ideas above.

_____

_____

_____

_____

_____

_____

_____

_____

_____

THE STORY: THE ORANGE AND THE SISTERS

There once were two sisters who lived in a house. Both sisters were very headstrong and set in their ways. Occasionally, they would get into arguments over who would make decisions about house repairs, food costs, and living arrangements. The older they got, the more they fought over issues.

One morning they were in the kitchen. When one of them opened the refrigerator, they noticed there was one orange left. Both sisters said they wanted the orange. For several minutes each sister stated strongly that she wanted the orange and that she deserved it more than the other. This went on for close to an hour.

Finally, to settle the argument, they decided to cut the orange in half. One sister cut it in half and the other sister chose first. Each sister took her half to opposite ends of the kitchen. One sister immediately peeled her half and ate the inside of the orange. The other sister was making a cake. She peeled her half of the orange and used the rind for flavoring in the cake and frosting.

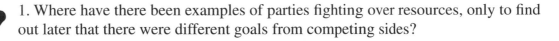

QUESTIONS TO CONSIDER

1. Where have there been examples of parties fighting over resources, only to find out later that there were different goals from competing sides?

2. Have there been hard confrontations in the past that ended in Pyrrhic (costly) victories? Describe.

3. Identify and discuss examples of conversation positively changing outcomes so that anger and resentment were lessened and relationships preserved and strengthened.

4. What lessons can our organization learn from the two sisters?

WHAT IF ...

1. The sisters were not so headstrong?

2. An orange and an apple were left?

NOTES TO MYSELF

_____

_____

_____

_____

_____

_____

_____

_____

_____

BALANCE: PAYING ATTENTION TO LIFE

We think often of the frantic, frenetic experiences of teachers and administrators and the cumulative effects of "running on empty." We've all experienced that. We get cranky, pessimistic, inflexible, short-tempered, and shortsighted. These are clearly not good ingredients to add to the pressure cooker of the 21st-century school. Our ability to respond creatively, with humor and insight, is limited. Crankiness, pessimism, rigidity, etc., tend to strain relationships, isolate people, and make life more difficult when this environment persists.

An important key here is balance. What do we mean by balance? I think everyone needs to have a quiet place in life. It could be any of a number of things – a quiet lake home, a secluded and personal room, a time when everyone is gone (and the TV is off).

What happens in stillness is that the subtle voices, the wellsprings, the inspirations that are so important to life and are often drowned out by louder, more persistent sounds, are able to come to the surface. We recognize the importance and power of these stirrings. Quiet time provides an opening for reflective thought. During quiet times we can see patterns as well. Sometimes the discovery or observation of patterns in one's life is the first step to healthy growth or change.

It also seems to us that balance includes the necessity of eating well and not as much. We've observed that much eating in schools at meetings is nervous, reactive. It's almost as if people tell themselves they feel so bad that they owe themselves a cookie to feel better, even though they know that the likely long-term consequences of one cookie after another are obesity and heart disease.

There was a time when a good friend of mine and I would find ourselves at meetings together. We'd tell each other as we approached the cookie tray that, though they looked good, cookies never tasted as good as we thought they would. The short spurt of energy would invariably be followed by a letdown.

There isn't much support for a healthy, balanced lifestyle in school. We can't really say why. Perhaps it's that bad food, cheap food, is so easy to come by in our society that it's easier to access junk food than healthy fruit or juice. Perhaps it's just being thoughtless rather than thoughtful.

The bottom line is that we have to make up our minds that balance and health are the most important factors in work and life. Choosing to make things balanced is a discipline, just like going for a walk or to the health club. We might help one another by walking in the halls before or after school, even talking as we walk, about issues like students, lessons, or other organizational matters. We've got to start providing healthful, low-fat alternatives to people in school: bagels and jelly, not donuts; juice, tea, and other natural drinks, not soda pop. And remember that all of this doesn't have to be perfect to be useful.

We've been focusing here on food in relation to balance. But there are many other areas of life as well where reflection about balance can be fruitful. For example, all of us would do well to seek balance in such matters as:

- Talking too much or too little.
- Sleeping too much or not enough.
- Worrying too much or too little about money.
- Being too harsh or too lenient with students.
- Working too many hours or not enough.
- Frequently getting advice from many different sources or virtually never listening to anyone.

You get the idea.

Sometimes doing one thing different is the key. Look at the week or the month and endeavor to make one thing different – healthier, more movement-oriented, more relaxing, more positive, more optimistic. If we all pitch in, the difference will be palpable and sustainable. Perhaps, then, we can restore some of the main casualties of the out-of-balance work life: health, hope, energy, passion, vibrancy, vitality.

 ## RESOURCES FOR DEEPER UNDERSTANDING

♦ ARTICLES

NSDC (National Staff Development Council) Library: Time for Staff Development. Found at >http://nsdc.org/educatorindex.htm<

Time has been used to structure what happens in schools, both in and out of the classroom. How can time be shaped to serve improvement efforts? How can teachers find time for their learning? How do alternative schedules affect student learning? This selection of resources will help you explore the issue of time and help with learning strategies to use time wisely.

Besides the NSDC articles listed below, you also will find links to other Websites, time-use research studies, and time-use strategies.

Barkley, Stephen. (1999). Time: it's made, not found. *Journal of Staff Development.* Fall.

Darling-Hammond, Linda. (1999). Target time toward teachers. *Journal of Staff Development.* Spring.

Guskey, Thomas R. (1999). Apply time with wisdom. *Journal of Staff Development.* Spring.

Hirsh, Stephanie. (1997). Investing the time to learn. *Results.* October.

How can schools make time for teacher learning? (1999). *Results.* March.

Killion, Joellen. (1999). Time for adult learning must connect to student learning. *Results.* May.

Member survey. (2001). NSDC.

Murphy, Carlene. (1997). Finding time for faculties to study together. *Journal of Staff Development.* Summer.

Pardini, Priscilla. (1999). Making time for adult learning. *Journal of Staff Development.* Spring.

Peterson, Kent D. (1999). Time use flows from school culture. *Journal of Staff Development.* Spring.

Richardson, Joan. (1997). Smart use of time and money enhances staff development. *Journal of Staff Development.* Winter.

Richardson, Joan. (1999). World-class learning: making the best even better. *Results.* November.

Sparks, Dennis. (2001). Time for professional learning serves student learning. *Results.* November.

The balancing act of adult life. *ERIC Digest.* Found at >http://www.ericfacility.net/ericdigests/ed459323.html<

♦ **THE BOOKSHELF**

Albom, Mitch. (1997). *Tuesdays with Morrie.* New York, NY: Doubleday.

Catford, Lorna, & Ray, Michael. (1991). *The Path of the Everyday Hero.* Los Angeles, CA: Jeremy Tarcher.

Covey, Stephen R., Merrill, A. Roger, & Merrill, Rebecca R. (1994). *First Things First.* New York, NY: Simon & Schuster.

Fassel, Diane. (1990). *Working Ourselves to Death.* New York, NY: HarperCollins.

Gardner, John W. (1963). *Self-Renewal.* New York, NY: Harper & Row.

Goodman, Joel. (1995). *Laffirmations.* Deerfield Beach, FL: Health Communications.

Hanh, Thich Nhat. (1975). *The Miracle of Mindfulness.* Boston, MA: Beacon Press.

Lustbader, Wendy. (2001). *What's Worth Knowing.* New York, NY: Penguin Putnam.

Palmer, Parker. (1998). *The Courage to Teach.* San Francisco, CA: Jossey-Bass.

Rivers, Frank. (1996). *The Way of the Owl.* San Francisco, CA: HarperCollins.

Sergiovanni, Thomas J. (1992). *Moral Leadership.* San Francisco, CA: Jossey-Bass.

♦ **USEFUL QUOTATIONS**

Things that matter most must never be at the mercy of things that matter least.
                    –Johann Wolfgang von Goethe, German writer and philosopher

You've got to think about "big things" while you're doing small things, so that all the small things go in the right direction.
                    –Alvin Toffler, U.S. business futurist and writer

Many people assume that they can probably find many ways to save time. This is an incorrect assumption for it is only when you focus on spending time that you begin to use your time effectively.
                    –Merrill Douglass, U.S. writer and speaker

Time is the scarcest resource, and unless it is managed, nothing else can be managed.
                    –Peter Drucker, Austrian/U.S. author and business consultant

It is always amazing how many of the things we do will never be missed. And nothing is less productive than to make more efficient what should not be done at all.
                    –Peter Drucker

The little things? The little moments? They aren't little.

> –John Kabat-Zinn, U.S. professor and author

Man always travels along precipices. His truest obligation is to keep his balance.

> –John Paul II, Roman Catholic pontiff

My object in living is to unite my avocation and my vocation
As my two eyes make one in sight.

> –Robert Frost, U.S. poet

Balance is the perfect state of still water. Let that be our model. It remains quiet within and is not disturbed on the surface.

> –Confucius, Chinese philosopher

Live a balanced life – learn some and think some and draw and paint and sing and dance and play and work every day some.

> –Robert Fulghum, U.S. social essayist

The essence of health is inner balance.

> –Andrew Weil, US. physician and writer

A man is born gentle and weak. At his death he is hard and stiff.
Green plants are tender and filled with sap. At their death they are withered and dry.
Therefore the stiff and unbending is the disciple of death.
The gentle and yielding is the disciple of life.
Thus an army without flexibility never wins a battle.
A tree that is unbending is easily broken.
The hard and strong will fall.
The soft and weak will overcome.

> –Lao Tzu, Chinese philosopher

Despite the encouraging and wonderful gains and the changes for women which have occurred in my lifetime, there is still room to advance and to promote correction of the remaining deficiencies and imbalances.

> –Sandra Day O'Connor, U.S. Supreme Court justice

There is more to life than increasing its speed.

> –Mahatma Gandhi, Indian philosopher and social activist

The sooner you fall behind, the more time you'll have to catch up.

> –Steven Wright, U.S. comedian

The gem cannot be polished without friction, nor man perfected without trials.

> –Chinese proverb

I shall be telling this with a sigh
Somewhere ages and ages hence;
Two roads diverged in a wood, and I –
I took the one less traveled by,
And that has made all the difference.

–Robert Frost

We shall not cease from exploration
And the end of all our exploring
Will be to arrive where we started
And know that place for the first time.

–T.S. Eliot, U.S. poet

Ultimately we know deeply that the other side of every fear is a freedom.
–Marilyn Ferguson, U.S. author

To follow your bliss is to live and work with passion and compassion.
–Lorna Catford and Michael Ray, U.S. professors and authors

Here's a test to find whether your mission on earth is finished: If you're alive, it isn't.
–Richard Bach, U.S. author

What lies beyond us and what lies before us are tiny matters when compared to what lies within us.
–Ralph Waldo Emerson, U.S. philosopher and writer

Never mistake knowledge for wisdom. One helps you make a living; the other helps you make a life.
–Sandra Carey, epigrammatist

Responsibility is our ability to respond to a situation. We always have a choice.
–Louise Hay, U.S. author

The only person who is going to make a change in your life is you.
–Louise Hay

When the student is ready, the teacher appears.
–Buddhist proverb

Soul doesn't pour into life automatically. It requires our skill and attention.
–Thomas Moore, U.S. psychotherapist and writer

THE BIG ROCKS OF LIFE

WHY THIS STORY?

The duties and expectations of educators are expanding at an alarming rate. Most educators are incredibly responsible adults who want more than anything to help make a positive difference in the lives of students. As we work longer and harder to meet increasingly unreasonable demands, we sacrifice or hold in abeyance some of the basic human needs (sleep, reflection, recreation, exercise, family).

Not long ago in the Memphis airport, Terminal A, I (Bill) saw a poster exhorting passersby to "Work on your non-work skills." For those of us who have difficulty moving away from our focus on work, the poster's five words might be helpful. The admonition changes the point of attention, so that if work is a major value in our lives, then to work on "non-work" might be a cutting edge for us. We would be living up to our values and, at the same time, bringing more balance to the overworked aspect of who we are.

Think for just a moment about some "non-work" that you want to do, then identify the skills needed for that non-work. Which of these skills might you develop so that your personal life-to-work ratio would be enhanced? If you're a work-oriented person, thinking of things to do to *prepare* for non-work might be a way to break the compulsive attention to work, a way to move into doing a larger percentage of non-work.

The only effective way to bring more balance to your personal life-to-work ratio is to make changes in your behaviors and beliefs – i.e., your values. As Curly says in the movie "City Slickers," you have to decide what the most important thing in life is.

〰〰〰〰〰〰〰〰〰〰

Begin by reading the story yourself. Decide whether you will use the story in your training. Make some notes about how the story does or does not fit with your work at this time. You also might want to expand on the ideas above.

_____

_____

_____

_____

_____

THE STORY: THE BIG ROCKS

One day an expert in time management was speaking to a group of business students and, to drive home a point, he used an illustration. Standing in front of the group of high-powered overachievers (read: hardworking educators) he said, "OK, time for a quiz."

He pulled out a one-gallon, wide-mouthed Mason jar and set it on the table in front of him. Then he produced about a dozen fist-sized rocks and carefully placed them, one at a time, into the jar. When the jar was filled to the top and no more rocks would fit inside, he asked, "Is this jar full?"

Everyone in the class said, "Yes."

He said, "Really?"

He then reached under the table and pulled out a bucket of gravel. He dumped some gravel in and shook the jar, causing 20 pieces of gravel to work themselves down into the spaces between the big rocks. Then he asked the group once more, "Is the jar full?"

By this time the class was on to him. "Probably not," one of them answered.

"Good!" he replied.

He reached under the table and brought out a bucket of sand. He started dumping the sand in the jar and it went into all of the spaces left between the rocks and the gravel. Once more he asked the question, "Is this jar full?"

"No!" the class shouted.

Once again he said, "Good." Then he grabbed a pitcher of water and began to pour it in until the jar was filled to the brim. Then he looked at the class and asked, "What is the point of this illustration?"

One eager beaver raised his hand and said, "The point is, no matter how full your schedule is, if you try really hard you can always fit some more things in it!"

"No," the speaker replied, "that's not the point.

"The truth this illustration teaches us is this: If you don't put the big rocks in first, you'll never get them in at all.

"What are the 'big rocks' in your life?" the speaker continued. "Your children. Your loved ones. Your education. Your dreams. A worthy cause. Teaching or mentoring others. Doing things you love. Time for yourself. Your health. Your life partner.

"Remember to put these *big rocks* in first, or you'll never get them in at all. If you sweat the small stuff – the gravel, sand, and water – you'll fill your life with little things that don't really matter, and all too seldom will you have the real quality time you need to spend on the big, important stuff – the big rocks.

"So … when you're reflecting on this little story, ask yourself this question: *What are the 'big rocks' in my life?* Then, put those in your jar first."

 **QUESTIONS TO CONSIDER**

1. What thoughts and feelings did you notice in yourself as the story unfolded?

2. What point would the speaker want us to remember? Where and how should we remember it?

3. If we got the story's point and began to put it into practice in a consistent manner, what would we be doing, saying, experiencing, thinking?

4. Are there any "dangers" in the story's message? If so, what are they? How important are they? How would you deal with them?

5. How would you describe a community whose culture included the "big rocks" philosophy? What might you observe?

6. How much control do we have – or not have – over filling our jar? How have we managed the process of filling our jar?

7. What are some of the "big rocks" that need to be in the jar? Examples of gravel? Sand? Water?

8. How do we reach agreement within learning communities about the "big rocks"?

WHAT IF ...

1. There are many more small rocks in your life than big ones?

2. There are not many rocks in your life?

NOTES TO MYSELF

_____

_____

_____

_____

_____

_____

1,000 MARBLES

WHY THIS STORY?

The balance between work and personal life is one of the most difficult issues facing leaders. The demands of our positions, especially in education, far exceed the available time, money, and energy. All over the country, there are shortages of candidates for leadership positions in school districts. Principals and superintendents are getting more and more difficult to find. When people are found, burnout is high.

So … how do we help committed leaders remain healthy? (The same type of question, by the way, also is being asked regarding pastors, priests and other religious leaders where burnout is quite high.) For the most part these are reasonable people who came into a profession to make a difference for students and families. They did not come into the profession to sacrifice body, mind, and soul. Granted, part of the solution lies in redesigning the work and making external community members aware of the demands, but another part of the answer is to help those in leadership positions focus on issues of balance, including the importance of having a fulfilling personal life.

We offer this story as a conversation starter for leaders, educators, support staff, and anyone else who is seeking balance between work life and personal life.

Begin by reading the story yourself. Decide whether you will use the story in your training. Make some notes about how the story does or does not fit with your work at this time. You also might want to expand on the ideas above.

_____

_____

_____

_____

_____

_____

_____

THE STORY: 1,000 MARBLES

The older I get, the more I enjoy Saturday mornings. Perhaps it's the quiet solitude that comes with being the first to rise, or maybe it's the unbounded joy of not having to be at work. Either way, the first few hours of a Saturday morning I find the most enjoyable.

A few weeks ago, I was shuffling toward the basement with a steaming cup of coffee in one hand and the morning paper in the other. What began as a typical Saturday morning turned into one of those lessons that life seems to hand you from time to time. Let me tell you about it.

I turned the dial of my ham radio up into the phone portion of the band in order to listen to a Saturday morning swap net. Along the way, I came across an older-sounding chap with a great signal and a golden voice. You know the kind: a voice *made* for broadcasting.

He was talking to someone named Tom about "a thousand marbles." I was intrigued and stopped to listen to what he had to say. It went something like this:

"Well, Tom, it sure sounds like you're busy with your job. I'm sure they pay you well, but it's a shame you have to be away from home and your family so much. Hard to believe a young fellow should have to work 60 or 70 hours a week to make ends meet.

"Too bad you missed your daughter's dance recital." He continued, "Let me tell you something, Tom, something that has helped me keep a good perspective on my own priorities."

That's when he began to explain his theory of a "thousand marbles." "You see," he said, "I sat down one day and did a little math. The average person lives about 75 years. I know, some live more and some live less, but on average, folks live about 75 years.

"Now then, I multiplied 75 by 52, and I came up with 3,900, which is the number of Saturdays that the average person has in their entire lifetime.

"Now bear with me, Tom, I'm getting to the important part. It took me until I was 55 years old to think about all of this in any detail, and by that time I had lived through over 2,800 Saturdays. I got to thinking that if I lived to be 75, I'd only have about a thousand of them left to enjoy.

"So I went to a toy store and bought every single marble they had. I ended up having to visit three toy stores to round up 1,000 marbles. I took them home and put them inside a clear plastic container right here next to my gear. Every Saturday since then I have taken one marble out and thrown it away. I've found that, by watching the marbles diminish, I focus more on the really important things in life.

"There is nothing like watching your time here on this earth run out to help get your priorities straight. Now let me tell you one last thing before I sign off and take my lovely wife out for breakfast. This morning I took the very last marble out of the container. I figure that if I make it until next Saturday then I have been given a little extra time. And the one thing we can all use is a little more time.

"It was nice to meet you, Tom. I hope you spend more time with your family, and I hope to meet you again here on the band. Seventy-five-year-old man, this is K9NZQ, clear and going QRT, good morning!"

You could have heard a pin drop on the band when this fellow signed off. I guess he gave us all a lot to think about. I had planned to work on the antenna that morning, after which I was going to meet up with a few hams to work on the next club newsletter.

Instead, I went upstairs and woke my wife up with a kiss. "C'mon, honey, I'm taking you and the kids out to breakfast."

"What brought this on?" she asked with a smile.

"Oh, it's just been a long time since we spent a Saturday together with the kids. Hey, can we stop at a toy store while we're out? I need to buy some marbles …"

QUESTIONS TO CONSIDER

1. What are you enjoying more as you get older? How do "quiet solitude" and "the unbounded joy of not having to be at work" resonate with you?

2. What have you discovered or been surprised about lately?

3. Reflect for a moment on your priorities and how you spend your time. How healthy or congruent are your priorities, as well as your choices in actually following through on those priorities?

4. What is the message here, and how does it relate to us in our work?

5. Think of two or three people who you think have successfully balanced their work and personal life. How did they do it? What changes did they have to make?

6. What are some goals that you want to reach by the time the last marble is taken out of the bowl? What changes are you willing to make in order to achieve those goals?

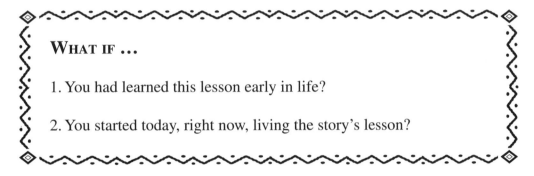

WHAT IF ...

1. You had learned this lesson early in life?

2. You started today, right now, living the story's lesson?

NOTES TO MYSELF

_____

_____

_____

_____

_____

_____

_____

_____

RULE NUMBER 6

WHY THIS STORY?

We wonder how often difficulties are caused by or related to the lack of balance in one's life or perspective. We think, as do many experts, that quite often they are. Too much time spent being upset or angry decreases your ability to think and takes a cumulative toll on your health.

This story is a gentle reminder of the importance of humor, even lighthearted self-deprecation, in one's life. It nudges us to a broader perspective and elicits humility. There's a recognition that the world will go on quite nicely without us (someone once said that "graveyards are full of indispensable people") and that enjoyment of life in the face of adversity is vitally important. In these chaotic, troubling times we need to calm down, take a deep breath, and put our lives and efforts in perspective. While our challenges are daunting, it's almost paradoxical to realize that the most effective way to meet them is by lightening up.

Begin by reading the story yourself. Decide whether you will use the story in your training. Make some notes about how the story does or does not fit with your work at this time. You also might want to expand on the ideas above.

_____

_____

_____

_____

_____

_____

_____

_____

_____

_____

THE STORY: RULE NUMBER 6

Two prime ministers are sitting in a room discussing affairs of state. Suddenly a man bursts in, apoplectic with fury, shouting and stamping and banging his fist on the desk. The resident prime minister admonishes him: "Peter," he says, "kindly remember Rule Number 6," whereupon Peter is instantly restored to complete calm, apologizes, and withdraws.

The politicians return to their conversation, only to be interrupted yet again twenty minutes later by an hysterical woman gesticulating wildly, her hair flying. Again the intruder is greeted with the words: "Marie, please remember Rule Number 6." Complete calm descends once more, and she too withdraws with a bow and an apology.

When the scene is repeated a third time, the visiting prime minister addresses his colleague: "My dear friend, I've seen many things in my life, but never anything as remarkable as this. Would you be willing to share with me the secret of Rule Number 6?"

"Very simple," replies the resident prime minister. "Rule Number 6 is 'Don't take yourself so goddamn seriously.'"

"Ah," says his visitor, "that is a fine rule."

After a moment of pondering, he inquires, "And what, may I ask, are the other rules?"

"There aren't any."

QUESTIONS TO CONSIDER

1. Think of and relate a time recently at work where you had a good laugh. How was it related to not taking yourself so seriously?

2. As you look at your work life, where do you see some possibility for gains in productivity by not taking yourself so blankety-blank seriously?

3. Are there people where you work who are especially gifted at not taking themselves so seriously? Describe how they act. What can we learn from them?

4. How can we remind ourselves on a more regular basis to be a little less intense about our efforts? What impact will this have on our work?

WHAT IF ...

1. There were other important rules? What might they be?

2. Rule Number 6 were applied more often?

NOTES TO MYSELF

_____

_____

_____

_____

_____

_____

_____

_____

_____

THE STORY OF THE FIVE BALLS

WHY THIS STORY?

This story is another that can help with the work/life balance. The work of an educator is characterized by never being done; that probably will not change in the short run. Given the pressures in education, it's delightful to be honored and noticed for hard work. Staff members report feeling less guilt about making their personal lives a priority when they hear leaders say that family and health are important too.

We think this story is also about integrity. Leaders need to know that integrity is enormously important, especially in the politically charged atmosphere we live in. Education, like a few other professions as well, has been trying to stand on ethical grounds even in the face of a blame-and-shame mentality. We think principled and ethical educators should be publicly honored more often.

Begin by reading the story yourself. Decide whether you will use the story in your training. Make some notes about how the story does or does not fit with your work at this time. You also might want to expand on the ideas above.

_____

_____

_____

_____

_____

_____

_____

_____

_____

THE STORY: THE STORY OF THE FIVE BALLS

Imagine life is a game in which you are juggling five balls. The balls are called work, family, health, friends, and integrity. And you're keeping all of them in the air. But one day you finally come to understand that work is a rubber ball. If you drop it, it will bounce back. The other four balls – family, health, friends, and integrity – are made of glass. If you drop one of these, it will be irrevocably scuffed, nicked, perhaps even shattered. And once you truly understand the lesson of the five balls, you will have the beginnings of balance in your life.

QUESTIONS TO CONSIDER

1. Which of the five balls is easiest to keep in the air?

2. Have any of your four glass balls been damaged? How?

3. Which of the balls needs more work or attention?

4. What are some ways you can make sure the balls that need the most attention get it?

5. Which ball do you feel most comfortable with?

WHAT IF ...

1. You don't experience the work ball as a rubber ball? What if it's something else, like a balloon filled with sand?

2. Other balls should be in the air? What might they be?

NOTES TO MYSELF

_____

_____

_____

_____

_____

_____

_____

_____

_____

_____

THE MILLER, HIS SON, AND THEIR DONKEY

WHY THIS STORY?

Mark Twain once said that the worst vice is advice! We agree. We're bombarded constantly with advice about how to do things – whether it's running a school, teaching a subject, relating to a student, or coaching a team.

While most of it is well-intentioned, the proffered advice has a curious consequence for educators. Because so much advice is given so often, educators can become confused. In addition, there really isn't time, given the pressures and demands of the job, to fully understand – let alone implement – the ideas. Confusion and overload develop. In the end, precious time and energy are wasted instead of being applied to areas that will make a difference.

We aren't saying that educators should hunker down, close the doors, and refuse to listen to what others are saying about schools. On the contrary, it's important to listen. (See the note on this point – last bulleted item – at the outset of this section on balance.) We emphasize, however, that it's essential to know who you are, what you value, and what you practice as a professional and school community – and not lose sight of what you know when copious and contradictory ideas are offered.

The story suggests that there's value in having the courage of your convictions. If there's a problem, at least it will be in response to difficulties *you* crafted. It seems to us there is excitement and animation there.

Begin by reading the story yourself. Decide whether you will use the story in your training. Make some notes about how the story does or does not fit with your work at this time. You also might want to expand on the ideas above.

_____

_____

_____

_____

_____

 ## THE STORY: THE MILLER, HIS SON, AND THEIR DONKEY

A miller, his son, and their donkey were walking from one town to another, hoping to find someone to buy the donkey; they couldn't afford to feed it during the approaching winter.

They hadn't gone far when they passed some travelers heading the other way. As they passed, the miller overheard one of the travelers say, "Look at those fools. With such a healthy donkey, one of them could surely ride."

Not wanting to appear foolish, the miller made his son mount the animal while the miller walked alongside.

After a while, they passed an inn. A group of old men sat in the sidewalk cafe sipping coffee, talking enthusiastically. As the miller and his son passed, an old man was overheard to say, "It's just as I've been telling you. The young are lazy and disrespectful of their elders. Look at that healthy boy riding the donkey while his old father walks!"

Again, not wishing to appear foolish or disrespectful himself, the miller asked his son to get off the donkey and climbed on.

They next met some women coming from town. "Why!" they cried. "Your poor little boy is nearly tired out. How can you ride and make him walk?"

Stinging from the criticism, the miller ordered his son to mount the donkey as they both rode.

"Would you believe it!" said another traveler to his companions. "This man is trying to kill his donkey. The poor thing will be exhausted, carrying such a heavy load. What a way to treat an animal!"

The miller and his son, not wanting to appear cruel, got off the donkey. The miller found some rope and a strong pole and, with his son's help, tied the donkey, upside down, to the pole. Then they carried the donkey on their shoulders.

As they got to town, people came out to witness this ridiculous spectacle. A crowd gathered, laughing, pointing fingers, and shouting. The crowd pressed in closer. As the trio crossed a bridge that led to town, the laughter and shouting so unnerved the donkey that it started to thrash around.

The animal struggled so much that the miller and his son could no longer hold it, and the donkey fell off the bridge into the water. The unfortunate donkey drowned, and the miller and his son had to walk all the way home, poorer than they were when they had started their journey. In trying to please everyone, they pleased no one, not even themselves.

QUESTIONS TO CONSIDER

1. What do you make of this story, and why should we pay attention to it?

2. What are some of the conflicting or contradictory messages coming to us in education? How do we best handle these messages?

3. To what extent do we respond like the miller? What specific shapes do these responses take? Examples?

4. What should the miller have done and why?

5. What should we in education do and why?

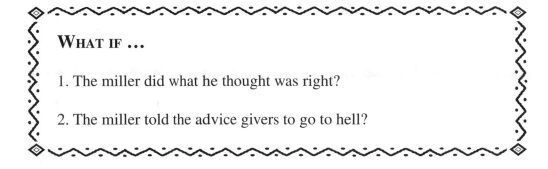

WHAT IF ...

1. The miller did what he thought was right?

2. The miller told the advice givers to go to hell?

NOTES TO MYSELF

_____

_____

_____

_____

_____

_____

_____

_____

_____

CHANGE: BENDING GRACEFULLY IN THE WIND

"Change" is a word with so much baggage that we wonder if we can still talk about it productively. For some, it's pejorative, while others find it exciting, even exhilarating. Not surprisingly, like most educators, we have great ambivalence about it. That said, change is a paradoxical, ubiquitous fact of life, requiring us to stay flexible, nimble, and (yes) humble.

Many hard feelings cluster around the idea of change. Misunderstandings result in our rushing to solutions without first discerning the dynamics of the situation and proposed changes. Those who favor the changes become "agents of change" while those who raise questions or disagree are labeled "change-averse" – such is the way of the value-laden word.

A refreshing idea has emerged from Robert Kegan and Lisa Laskow Lahey in an article in the *Harvard Business Review* called "The Real Reason People Don't Change." According to the authors, people don't change because they have competing, mutually exclusive commitments. While I may be committed to change, I know I must maintain some order in the school and classroom, or chaos will sabotage learning. Gaining insight into competing personal commitments and values can facilitate change. We are, after all, involved in a complicated balancing act that includes important issues like safety, values, judgments, commitments, and strongly held ideas about the way of the world. What's refreshing is that Kegan and Lahey offer a way to think about change in dynamically fluid situations without harsh judgments or condemnation.

It strikes us that in many ways the concept of change is a red herring, obscuring deeper issues like community values and the benefits of working together for a common good. The debate over whether I should adopt change deflects deeper conversations we should be having – and personalizes an issue that should not be personalized. It introduces an element into our relationships that ironically threatens our ability *to* change, progress, and continually improve. We begin to doubt our collective ability to change appropriately in response to new circumstances, our ability to do what is best for our future together.

Greek philosopher Heraclitus said, "You can't step in the same river twice." Education is like a river, running ever faster and faster. Management professor and change theorist Peter Vaill uses the metaphor of being in permanent whitewater rapids. Most administrators and teachers we know feel as if they're traveling through whitewater most of the time.

So ... how do you navigate your way through whitewater where change is the norm and the pace of change is quickening? One way is by preparing staff to talk about change. Ignoring the reality of change doesn't work. These stories can set the tone for dealing productively with change.

We also strongly encourage you to seek further resources about change, specifically the work of Shirley Hord and Gene Hall, educational authors and consultants. Their work has been available for many years and has proven to be extremely helpful with change management.

 ## RESOURCES FOR DEEPER UNDERSTANDING

♦ ARTICLES

Janas, Monica. (1998). Shhh ... the dragon is asleep and its name is resistance. *Journal of Staff Development.* Summer.

Kegan, Robert, & Lahey, Lisa Laskow. (2001). The real reason people won't change. *Harvard Business Review.* November.

Resistance to change. NSDC (National Staff Development Council) Library. Found at >http://nsdc.org/educatorindex.htm<

Richardson, Joan. (1997). Dealing with resisters biggest challenge for staff developers. *Developer.* March.

Sparks, Dennis. (1997). Is resistance to change really the problem? *Developer.* March.

Sparks, Dennis. (2001). Why change is so challenging for schools: an interview with Peter Senge. *Journal of Staff Development.* Summer.

Supovitz, Jonathan, & Zief, Susan Goerlich. (2000). Why they stay away. *Journal of Staff Development.* Fall.

♦ THE BOOKSHELF

Barth, Roland S. (1990). *Improving Schools from Within.* San Francisco, CA: Jossey-Bass.

Bode, Richard. (1993). *First You Have to Row a Little Boat.* New York, NY: Warner Books.

Covey, Stephen R. (1989). *The Seven Habits of Highly Effective People.* New York, NY: Simon & Schuster.

Hall, Gene E., & Hord, Shirley M. (2001). *Implementing Change: Patterns, Principles, Potholes.* Upper Saddle River, NJ: Pearson Allyn & Bacon.

Hamel, Gary. (2002). *Leading the Revolution: How to Thrive in Turbulent Times by Making Innovation a Way of Life.* New York, NY: Plume.

Fullan, Michael. (2001). *Leading in a Culture of Change.* San Francisco, CA: Jossey-Bass.

Zander, Benjamin, & Zander, Rosamund Stone. (2000). *The Art of Possibility.* Boston, MA: Harvard Business School Press.

♦ **USEFUL QUOTATIONS**

People don't resist change. They resist being changed!
—Peter Senge, U.S. consultant and author

Change has a bad reputation in our society. But it isn't all bad – not by any means. In fact, change is necessary in life – to keep us moving ... to keep us growing ... to keep us interested ... Imagine life without change. It would be static ... boring ... dull.
—Dennis O'Grady, U.S. psychotherapist and newspaper columnist

It is a bad plan that admits of no modification.
—Publius Syrus, Roman epigrammatist

Never doubt that a small group of thoughtful, concerned citizens can change the world. Indeed, it is the only thing that ever has.
—Margaret Mead, U.S. anthropologist and writer

Company cultures are like country cultures. Never try to change one. Try, instead, to work with what you've got.
—Peter Drucker, Austrian/U.S. author and business consultant

Resistance to change does not reflect opposition, nor is it merely a result of inertia. Instead, even as they hold a sincere commitment to change, many people are unwittingly applying productive energy toward a hidden competing commitment. The resulting dynamic equilibrium stalls the effort in what looks like resistance but is in fact a kind of personal immunity to change.
—Robert Kegan and Lisa Laskow Lahey, U.S. business consultants and writers

You must be the change you wish to see in the world.
—Mahatma Gandhi, Indian philosopher and social activist

I am convinced that if the rate of change inside an organization is less than the rate of change outside, the end is in sight.
—Jack Welch, U.S. business executive and writer

The only completely consistent people are dead.

–Aldous Huxley, British writer

The illiterate of the future are not those who can't read or write but those who cannot learn, unlearn, and relearn.

–Alvin Toffler, U.S. business futurist and writer

When one door closes, another opens: But we often look so long and so regretfully upon the closed door that we do not see the one which has opened for us.

–Alexander Graham Bell, U.S. inventor

If you always do what you've always done, you'll always get what you've always got.

–Ed Foreman, U.S. motivational speaker

It's not so much that we're afraid of change or so in love with the old ways, but it's that place in between that we fear … It's like being between trapezes. It's Linus when his blanket is in the dryer. There's nothing to hold on to.

–Marilyn Ferguson, U.S. author

It isn't the changes that do you in, it's the transitions.

–William Bridges, U.S. consultant and author

Faced with the choice between changing one's mind and proving that there is no need to do so, almost everybody gets busy on the proof.

–John Kenneth Galbraith, Canadian/U.S. economist and writer

One doesn't discover new lands without consenting to lose sight of the shore for a very long time.

–André Gide, French novelist

Everyone thinks of changing the world, but no one thinks of changing himself.

–Leo Tolstoy, Russian novelist

There is a time for departure even when there's no certain place to go.

–Tennessee Williams, U.S. playwright

It doesn't work to leap a 20-foot chasm in two 10-foot jumps.

–North American proverb

We trained hard … but every time we were beginning to form up into teams, we would be reorganized. I was to learn later in life that we tend to meet any new situation by reorganizing … and a wonderful method it can be of creating the illusion of progress while producing inefficiency and demoralization.

–*Satyricon* (Petronius, Roman satirist)

An ounce of action is worth a ton of theory.

–Friedrich Engels, German philosopher and writer

Eliminate something superfluous from your life. Break a habit. Do something that makes you feel insecure. Carry out an action with complete attention and intensity, as if it were your last.

–Piero Ferrucci, Italian psychologist and author

If you don't like something, change it. If you can't change it, change your attitude. Don't complain.

–Maya Angelou, U.S. poet

Any change, even a change for the better, is always accompanied by drawbacks and discomforts.

–Arnold Bennett, British writer

It is not necessary to change. Survival is not mandatory.

–W. Edwards Deming, U.S. business adviser and author

Few will have the greatness to bend history itself; but each of us can work to change a small portion of events, and in the total of all those acts will be written the history of this generation.

–Robert F. Kennedy, U.S. senator and attorney general

All change is not growth; all movement is not forward.

–Ellen Glasgow, U.S. novelist

Creatures whose mainspring is curiosity enjoy the accumulating of facts far more than the pausing at times to reflect on those facts.

–Clarence Day, U.S. biographer and essayist

A great many people think they are changing when they are only rearranging their prejudices.

–James Baldwin, U.S./French writer

◈ THE GORILLA STORY ◈

WHY THIS STORY?

Change is irritating. It is confusing, mysterious, unsettling, yet undeniable. It knocks us off balance. It frequently pushes us beyond our comfort zones. We're compelled to run faster and faster just to keep up. And there's no end in sight, no resting.

Because of the nature of things, we have to abandon what isn't working. We must create new ways of being in the world and with each other. This is very demanding, energy-consuming work. We find ourselves reacting to changes proposed or demanded by others – parents, businesspeople, legislators, boards of education, et al. – while the real task, it seems to us, is to proactively create our future together. The alternative is to react defensively to changes being thrust upon us, thereby creating a future not chosen, into which we stumble, instead of a future we actively helped shape.

How do we react to change in our setting? Should we navigate a proposed change? If so, how? How do we keep the best of the old, yet be open to creating new, responsive, and intelligent practices and protocols? Is change inside or outside us? How do we do it best? And who defines change? How do we remain sane and civil while exploring our common future? And where do we find the time (not to mention energy) to investigate, consider, and create?

〰〰〰〰〰〰〰〰〰

Begin by reading the story yourself. Decide whether you will use the story in your training. Make some notes about how the story does or does not fit with your work at this time. You also might want to expand on the ideas above.

_____

_____

_____

_____

_____

_____

_____

THE STORY: THE GORILLA STORY

This story starts with a cage containing five gorillas and a large bunch of bananas hanging above some stairs in the center of the cage. Before long, a gorilla goes to the stairs and starts to climb toward the bananas. As soon as he touches the stairs, all the gorillas are sprayed with cold water. After a while, another gorilla makes an attempt and gets the same result – all the gorillas are sprayed with cold water. Every time a gorilla attempts to retrieve the bananas, the others are sprayed. Eventually, they quit trying and leave the bananas alone.

One of the original five gorillas is removed from the cage and replaced with a new one. The new gorilla sees the bananas and starts to climb the stairs. To his horror, all the other gorillas attack him. After another attempt and attack, he knows that if he tries to climb the stairs he will be assaulted. Next, the second of the original five gorillas is replaced with a new one. The newcomer goes to the stairs and is attacked. The previous newcomer takes part in the punishment with enthusiasm.

Next the third original gorilla is replaced with a new one. The new one goes for the stairs and is attacked as well. Two of the four gorillas that beat him have no idea why they were not permitted to climb the stairs or why they are participating in the beating of the newest gorilla.

After the fourth and fifth original gorillas have been replaced, all the gorillas that were sprayed with cold water are gone. Nevertheless, no gorilla will ever again approach the stairs. Why not?

"Because that's the way it has always been done."

QUESTIONS TO CONSIDER

1. What were your reactions to the story as it unfolded?

2. What point would the author want us to remember? To what extent does it apply to our work?

3. Describe some old ways and some new ways. What are some strengths and weaknesses of both the new and the old?

4. Explain any examples you can think of where the story plays out in our work.

5. What might have been good strategies for intervention in a system like the one in the story?

6. How could individuals act to make the situation healthier? In other words, how do you approach changing this culture?

7. A strong cultural component is forced onto newcomers in the story. How do we welcome newcomers into our school, and what messages do they get? How much is intentional? How much "just happens"?

WHAT IF ...

1. All the other gorillas cheered and supported the first gorilla?

2. One of the new gorillas asked what was going on?

NOTES TO MYSELF

_____

_____

_____

_____

_____

_____

_____

THE RABBI'S GIFT

WHY THIS STORY?

Having fallen on hard times ourselves, educators can relate to the plight of the monastery in the next story. Perhaps the time has come for us to be quiet and contemplative about who we are; it could be a time for questions more than answers. What do we value? How do we live those values? Maybe it's a time for us to look inward and to each other for the strength to keep going.

This story reinforces the importance of intention in our work. It reminds us of the necessity of being open and respectful to those who are different from us. Diversity and change are intimately intertwined, and we are mindful of the advice of Michael Fullan, Canadian consultant and author, to respect those you wish to silence.

Begin by reading the story yourself. Decide whether you will use the story in your training. Make some notes about how the story does or does not fit with your work at this time. You also might want to expand on the ideas above.

_____

_____

_____

_____

_____

_____

_____

_____

_____

_____

THE STORY: THE RABBI'S GIFT

This story concerns a monastery that had fallen upon hard times. Once a great order, as a result of waves of antimonastic persecution in the seventeenth and eighteenth centuries and the rise of secularism in the nineteenth, all its branch houses were lost and it had become decimated to the extent that there were only five monks left in the decaying mother house: the abbot and four others, all over seventy in age. Clearly it was a dying order.

In the deep woods surrounding the monastery there was a little hut that a rabbi from a nearby town occasionally used for a hermitage. Through their many years of prayer and contemplation the old monks had become a bit psychic, so they could always sense when the rabbi was in his hermitage. "The rabbi is in the woods, the rabbi is in the woods again," they would whisper to each other. As he agonized over the imminent death of his order, it occurred to the abbot at one such time to visit the hermitage and ask the rabbi if by some possible chance he could offer any advice that might save the monastery.

The rabbi welcomed the abbot at his hut. But when the abbot explained the purpose of his visit, the rabbi could only commiserate with him. "I know how it is," he exclaimed. "The spirit has gone out of the people. It is the same in my town. Almost no one comes to the synagogue anymore." So the old rabbi and the old abbot wept together. Then they read parts of the Torah and quietly spoke of deep things. The time came when the abbot had to leave. They embraced each other. "It has been a wonderful thing that we should meet after all these years," the abbot said, "but I have still failed in my purpose for coming here. Is there nothing you can tell me, no piece of advice you can give me that would help me save my dying order?"

"No, I am sorry," the rabbi responded, "I have no advice to give. The only thing I can tell you is that the Messiah is one of you."

When the abbot returned to the monastery his fellow monks gathered around him to ask, "Well, what did the rabbi say?"

"He couldn't help," the abbot answered. "We just wept and read the Torah together. The only thing he did say, just as I was leaving – it was something cryptic – was that the Messiah is one of us. I don't know what he meant."

In the days and weeks and months that followed, the old monks pondered this and wondered whether there was any possible significance to the rabbi's words. "The Messiah is one of us? Could he possibly have meant one of us monks here at the monastery? If that's the case, which one? Do you suppose he meant the abbot? Yes, if he meant anyone, he probably meant Father Abbot. He has been our leader for more than a generation. On the other hand, he might have meant Brother Thomas. Certainly Brother Thomas is a holy man. Everyone knows that Thomas is a man of light. Certainly he could not have meant Brother Elred! Elred gets crotchety at times. But come to think of it, even though he is a thorn in people's sides, when I look back on it, Elred is virtually always right. Often very right. Maybe the rabbi did mean Brother Elred. But surely not Brother Phillip. Phillip is so passive, a real nobody. But then, almost mysteriously, he has a gift for somehow always being there when you need him. He just magically appears by your side. Maybe Phillip is the Messiah. Of course the rabbi didn't mean me. He couldn't possibly have meant me. I'm just an ordinary person. Yet supposing he did? Suppose I am the Messiah? Oh God, not me. I couldn't be that much for You, could I?"

As they contemplated in this manner, the old monks began to treat each other with extraordinary respect on the off chance that one among them might be the Messiah. And on the off, off chance that each monk himself might be the Messiah, they began to treat themselves with extraordinary respect.

Because the forest in which it was situated was beautiful, it so happened that people still occasionally came to visit the monastery to picnic on its tiny lawn, to wander along some of its paths, even now and then to go into the dilapidated chapel to meditate. As they did so, without even being conscious of it, they sensed this aura of extraordinary respect that now began to surround the five old monks and seemed to radiate out from them and permeate the atmosphere of the place. There was something strangely attractive, even compelling, about it. Hardly knowing why, they began to come back to the monastery more frequently to picnic, to play, to pray. They began to bring their friends to show them this special place. And their friends brought their friends.

Then it happened that some of the younger men who came to visit the monastery started to talk more and more with the old monks. After a while one asked if he could join them. Then another. And another. So within a few years the monastery had once again become a thriving order and, thanks to the rabbi's gift, a vibrant center of light and spirituality in the realm.

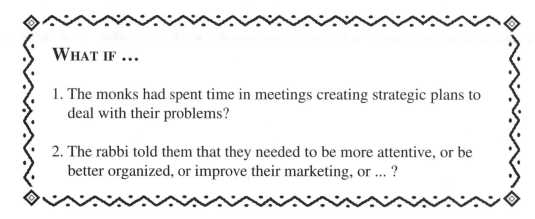

Questions to Consider

1. If we are building learning communities, what lessons can we draw from the story?

2. What specific behaviors in schools would reinforce this point of view?

3. How do we set aside or disarm judgments that keep us from treating each other with "extraordinary respect"?

4. Describe a time or times in your school or learning community where you've seen the dynamic of the story played out. What were positive and negative impacts? (For example, you might have taken time to listen to a person, but you failed to accomplish a task on time.)

5. How will you find out who is the savior among us?

What if ...

1. The monks had spent time in meetings creating strategic plans to deal with their problems?

2. The rabbi told them that they needed to be more attentive, or be better organized, or improve their marketing, or ... ?

Notes to Myself

_____

_____

_____

_____

_____

_____

_____

A SYSTEM TRAPPED

WHY THIS STORY?

We often see change as something that is imposed from the outside. We talk of change as an abstract construct outside of ourselves. We talk about it as an object removed from our circumstances. We characterize it as linear, planned, strategic. And for all our efforts, changes often haven't worked out very well.

In the process of change we are reminded how the power of our thoughts controls our actions. We notice as well the importance of agreeing on action as a community – and all the while building the protocols, procedures, and practices that create the institution we choose.

Clearly, change is difficult and requires extraordinary work. Productive change calls for an enormous amount of thought. It also compels us to take action. It takes effort to roll back the darkness. We're reminded of a quote our Canadian friend Patrick O'Neill uses in his "Extraordinary Conversations" training. He quotes Rumi, a medieval Persian poet and mystic: "To those whose job it is to wake the dead, get up! Today's a work day!"

Begin by reading the story yourself. Decide whether you will use the story in your training. Make some notes about how the story does or does not fit with your work at this time. You also might want to expand on the ideas above.

_____

_____

_____

_____

_____

_____

_____

_____

THE STORY: A SYSTEM TRAPPED

Like other industrial age institutions today, educational institutions are caught in extraordinary cross-currents of change. Businesses also struggle with increasing pressures for performance to please external stakeholders. They too create extraordinary stresses on their members by attempting to get more output while reducing head count.

Yet, as someone who spends considerable time with educators and businesspeople, it is my judgment that educators feel more trapped and less able to innovate than do their business counterparts. Several years ago I asked a group of educators a question I have often asked of business groups: "Do you believe that significant change occurs only as a result of a crisis?" In business groups, typically three-quarters will respond affirmatively [that crisis mandates change]. But, then, others will tell stories of significant changes that arose without a crisis, from passion and imagination, from leaders of many types willing to take risks in favor of something in which they believed. The group of educators responded differently. Very few raised their hands at my first question. Puzzled, I asked, "Does that mean that you believe that significant innovation can occur without crises?" None raised a hand in response to this question either. Now really puzzled, I asked: "Well, if change doesn't occur in response to a crisis, and it doesn't occur in the absence of a crisis, what other possibilities are there?" A soft voice from the audience responded, "I guess we don't believe significant change can occur under any circumstances." Those who have not worked within the institutions of education often do not appreciate just how disempowered educators feel.

QUESTIONS TO CONSIDER

1. To what extent is this an accurate description of the change process in education?

2. What impact does this description have on you? The profession? Schools?

3. What evidence or stories could you cite to support or disprove the speaker's point?

4. How important is it that adults – and educators in particular – feel that change is possible?

5. To what extent would an individual be able to counter this idea? To what extent could a team counter the idea?

6. What behaviors and supports are likely to increase the possibility of change?

WHAT IF ...

1. Change did occur in schools as a result of crisis? Change occurred in schools due to imagination and passion, not crisis?

2. Significant change occurred? What would it look like?

NOTES TO MYSELF

_____

_____

_____

_____

_____

_____

_____

_____

THE CHRYSALIS

WHY THIS STORY?

Learning is content and process. With the policymakers focusing on content knowledge and testing, we sometimes forget that learning is a process, and it takes time. U.S. consultants and authors Gene Hall and Shirley Hord said many years ago that "change is a process, not an event." Learning is change. After all, don't you have to admit you don't know something in order to learn it?

U.S. author and trainer Stephen Covey, in many of his works, uses the metaphor of farming to describe education and learning. You can't wait until July, then "cram" to start producing a crop. How many of us in school waited too long to study, then tried to cram right before the test? How did it work out for you? Learning is a natural process that takes time and can't be rushed.

This story shows that trying to hasten natural processes can have devastating consequences. Rushing nature may garner quick short-term rewards, with terrible long-term results. This dynamic is sometimes referred to as exchanging short-term gain for long-term pain. The axiom's inverse corollary ("short-term pain for long-term gain") tends to be more productive.

Begin by reading the story yourself. Decide whether you will use the story in your training. Make some notes about how the story does or does not fit with your work at this time. You also might want to expand on the ideas above.

_____

_____

_____

_____

_____

_____

_____

_____

THE STORY: THE CHRYSALIS

Once, I remembered, I had detached a chrysalis from the trunk of an olive tree and placed it in my palm. Inside the transparent coating I discerned a living thing. It was moving. The hidden process must have reached its terminus; the future, still-enslaved butterfly was waiting with silent tremors for the sacred hour when it would emerge into the sunlight. It was not in a hurry. Having confidence in the light, the warm air, in God's eternal law, it was waiting.

But I was in a hurry. I wanted to see the miracle hatch before me as soon as possible, wanted to see how the body surges out of its tomb and shroud to become a soul. Bending over, I began to blow my warm breath over the chrysalis, and behold! A slit soon incised itself on the chrysalis's back, the entire shroud gradually split from top to bottom, and the immature, bright green butterfly appeared, still tightly locked together, its wings twisted, its legs glued to its abdomen. It squirmed gently and kept coming more and more to life beneath my warm, persistent breath. One wing as pale as a budding poplar leaf disengaged itself from the body and began to palpitate, struggling to unfold along its entire length, but in vain. It stayed half opened, shriveled. Soon the other wing moved as well, toiled in its own right to stretch, was unable to, and remained half unfolded and trembling. I, with a human being's effrontery, continued to lean over and blow my warm exhalation upon the maimed wings, but they had ceased to move now and had drooped down, as stiff and lifeless as stone.

I felt sick at heart. Because of my hurry, because I had dared to transgress an eternal law, I had killed the butterfly. In my hand I held a carcass. Years and years have passed, but that butterfly's weightless carcass has weighed heavily on my conscience ever since.

1. What did you track internally as the story unfolded?

2. What point would the author want us to remember?

3. If we got the story's point and began to practice it in a consistent manner, what would we be doing, saying, experiencing, thinking?

4. Are there any "dangers" in this point of view? If so, what are they? How important are they? How would you deal with them?

5. How would you describe a community that in their culture has the values or perceptions of the author? What might you observe?

6. What aspects of the story are important to keep in mind in schools?

WHAT IF ...

1. The author refused to learn the lesson?

2. The butterfly responded, emerged, and flew off? What message would that have conveyed to the author and to us?

NOTES TO MYSELF

_____

_____

_____

_____

_____

_____

_____

AUTOBIOGRAPHY IN FIVE CHAPTERS

WHY THIS STORY?

Change is hard; have you noticed?! Our patterns get locked in as our ways of operating seem to work. But as time moves on, things change. Suddenly our standard operating procedures don't seem to work as well as they have in the past, or they aren't working at all. We tend to blame all kinds of causes, most of them external. Of course, when we step back, things are changing and will continue to do so.

This short story is meant to raise your awareness of what you're doing, get you to notice the results you're getting, and maybe, just maybe, show you that it could be worthwhile to consider other alternatives.

Begin by reading the story yourself. Decide whether you will use the story in your training. Make some notes about how the story does or does not fit with your work at this time. You also might want to expand on the ideas above.

_____

_____

_____

_____

_____

_____

_____

_____

_____

_____

THE STORY: AUTOBIOGRAPHY IN FIVE CHAPTERS

1) I walk down the street.
There is a deep hole in the sidewalk
I fall in.
I am lost ... I am hopeless.
It isn't my fault.
It takes forever to find a way out.

2) I walk down the same street.
There is a deep hole in the sidewalk
I pretend I don't see it.
I fall in again.
I can't believe I'm in the same place.
But it isn't my fault.
It still takes a long time to get out.

3) I walk down the same street.
There is a deep hole in the sidewalk
I see it is there.
I still fall in ... it's a habit
My eyes are open
I know where I am
It is *my* fault.
I get out immediately.

4) I walk down the same street.
There is a deep hole in the sidewalk
I walk around it.

5) I walk down another street.

Questions to Consider

1. What lesson(s) do you take from the story?

2. How does the story relate to education in general? Our work in schools?

3. What holes are we pretending not to see? Why? What is that all about?

4. What holes do we see and habitually fall in? Why? What is that about?

5. Describe other streets we have to walk down. In other words, what requires rethinking?

6. What holes are we walking around?

What if ...

1. You had company on your walk?

2. There were many distractions: cars driving (some erratically) on the street, children playing in your path, other pedestrians you have to avoid bumping into, or it's raining/snowing?

Notes to Myself

_____

_____

_____

_____

_____

_____

_____

_____

# STORY SOURCES

"'How Are the Children?'" (excerpted from speech by Rev. Patrick T. O'Neill): in public domain.

"My Grandfather's Story (Two Wolves)": adapted by authors after hearing it at Angeles Arrien workshop.

"The Twenty-Eighth Floor": Wydro, Kenneth. (1981). *Think on Your Feet: The Art of Thinking and Speaking Under Pressure.* Upper Saddle River, NJ: Prentice Hall.

"The Wooden Bowl": adapted from folk tale in public domain.

"Fire and Water": Kim, W. Chan, & Mauborgne, Renée A. (1992). Parables of leadership. *Harvard Business Review.* July-August.

"Cleaning Sidewalks": Oshry, Barry. (1995). *Seeing Systems: Unlocking the Mysteries of Organizational Life.* San Francisco: Berret-Koehler Publishers.

"The Animal School": Reavis, George H. In public domain.

"The Cracked Pot": folk tale in public domain.

"Two Hawks": adapted from story told by Edward de Bono at the 1991 International Conference on Thinking held at Massachusetts Institute of Technology.

"The Gabra": adapted from research of David Maybury-Lewis.

"Epilogue: A Soft Answer": Dobson, Terry. (1982). *Safe and Alive.* Los Angeles, CA: J.P. Tarcher.

"The Wind and the Sun": adapted from fable by Aesop.

"The Wisdom of the Mountain": Kim, W. Chan, & Mauborgne, Renée A. (1992). Parables of leadership. *Harvard Business Review.* July-August.

"Getting What You Want – The Other Way": in public domain.

"The Orange and the Sisters": adapted from story in public domain.

"The Big Rocks of Life": in public domain.

"1,000 Marbles": in public domain.

"Rule Number 6": Zander, Rosamund Stone, & Zander, Benjamin. (2000). *The Art of Possibility: TransformingProfessional and Personal Life*. Boston, MA: Harvard Business School Press.

"The Story of the Five Balls": Patterson, James. (2001). New York, NY: Little, Brown & Company.

"The Miller, His Son, and Their Donkey": adapted from fable by Aesop.

"The Gorilla Story": in public domain.

"The Rabbi's Gift": Peck, M. Scott. (1987). *The Different Drum: Community Making and Peace*. New York, NY: Simon & Schuster.

"A System Trapped": Senge, Peter. (1999) *Schools That Learn: A Fifth Discipline Fieldbook for Parents, Educators, and Everyone Who Cares About Education.* New York, NY: Doubleday.

"The Chrysalis": Kazantzakis, Nikos. English translation by Bien, P.A. (1985). New York, NY: Simon & Schuster.

"Autobiography in Five Chapters": Nelson, Portia. (1993). *There's a Hole in My Sidewalk: The Romance of Self-Discovery.* Hillsboro, OR: Beyond Words Publishing.